SOPHIE REDESIGNED

A SOPHIE AND SAM MYSTERY

KAREN DAHOOD

Outskirts Press, Inc.
Denver, Colorado

This is a work of fiction. The events and characters described herein are imaginary and are not intended to refer to specific places or living persons. The opinions expressed in this manuscript are solely the opinions of the author and do not represent the opinions or thoughts of the publisher. The author has represented and warranted full ownership and/or legal right to publish all the materials in this book.

Sophie Redesigned
A Sophie and Sam Mystery
All Rights Reserved.
Copyright © 2010 Karen Dahood
V3.0 R1.0

Cover Photo © 2010 JupiterImages Corporation. All rights reserved - used with permission.

This book may not be reproduced, transmitted, or stored in whole or in part by any means, including graphic, electronic, or mechanical without the express written consent of the publisher except in the case of brief quotations embodied in critical articles and reviews.

Outskirts Press, Inc.
http://www.outskirtspress.com

ISBN: 978-1-4327-5344-3

Outskirts Press and the "OP" logo are trademarks belonging to Outskirts Press, Inc.

PRINTED IN THE UNITED STATES OF AMERICA

ACKNOWLEDGMENTS & APPRECIATIONS

Sally Dahood, my mother-in-law, was the inspiration for the Sophie George mystery series when I started sketching them out in 1986. Early on in her life she had disowned her given name, Sophie, because cruel kids would chant, "Sophie, Sophie, big fat sofa." She was in fact petite – but a very big influence on her two sons and everyone else who got to know her. Just like the fictional Sophie, she was very smart, despite the fact her father would not give her money to buy pencils and tablets to continue her schooling. At a very young age she started to work to help her mother pay the bills. When I met her, she was a widow, living in Florida on her investments.

The real Sophie/Sally was never a librarian. That idea came from the several years I worked alongside librarians on National Endowment funded library programs. Librarians need all the publicity and thanks they can get. Last year I discovered the "Gladdy Gold" mysteries. Rita Lakin's sleuth also is a retired librarian. Perhaps that accomplished author has similar appreciation for those wonderful, unsung educators. Perhaps all writers do.

Since I am a product of academic writing programs, I was averse to self-publishing until I attended the Tony Hillerman Mystery Writers Conference in 2008, and was impressed by two very important changes: one is that the publishing industry was undergoing a revolution, due in part to Kindle; the other is that authors now have to be entrepreneurs. Therefore, I returned to my original purpose (discouraged by agents), to weave a subtext of life review and lessons for aging into the fabric of entertainment, and to associate with others who think aging can be better than it is.

Sophie George lives in a condo retirement community on the west coast of Florida. Gladdy Gold lives in a multi-story retirement complex on the east coast of Florida. I live in Arizona where "active retirement" has been a magnet for in-migration. It's when people become less active that problems – physical, emotional, mental, financial – show up, and those kinds of problems have driven my stories. If you go to my website www.moxiecosmos.com you will find discussion questions for SOPHIE REDESIGNED and a lively discussion among eldercare workers on the MoxieCosmos blog.

So, thank you to Trinity Demask at Outskirts Press for holding my hand through this process, and to Morella Bierwag (mo@letsgocommunications.com), website genius and sympathetic partner to this project because she is the eldercare volunteer in her family. Thanks also to my illustrator, Jodi Netzer, a young graphic artist, dancer, poet, and community organizer, and to Will Seberger, the globe-trotting photo-journalist who managed to make me look energetic without erasing my well-earned wrinkles.

This book is dedicated to three of our grandchildren, Sophia Woodruff and her cousins Max and Emilie Fisher, who kindly did their homework and played beside their elderly great-grandmother when she became frail and lonely, and even as she lay dying in her room in our home. These children will know how to mature with vision, courage, and gratitude for every day of their lives.

Karen Dahood
Tucson 2009

FIRST WEEK

Friday, June 12, 1998

To beat the crowd, I always finish my two mile walk at the crossroads of Dorado Place and Dorado Circle by 7 a.m. On this particular day I saw a strange car backing out of the driveway at Deborah Conyers' house on Dorado Place, a cul de sac. Since she is a man's kind of woman, I wasn't too surprised. I hugged the shrubbery to let it pass. It was long and shiny black. Then I noticed the tinted windows, almost like a hearse, and felt a cold shudder run up my back that had nothing to do with the early morning air. It was the reminder that just months ago we buried Hank, Deborah's long time beau. She was so obviously heartsick that I had wondered how long she could survive without him. Just to be sure, I walked up to her front door intending to knock lightly. Normally she would not be receiving visitors this early in the morning. The door was wide open. I realized I should have looked at that car's license plate.

To my relief, Deborah was safe, standing in front of a long oval mirror that was the centerpiece in her tiny foyer. She didn't see me when I paused at her stoop. She switched on the wall sconces at either side of the mirror and leaned forward to seriously scrutinize her face. From where I stood, I could see her reflection. There was something very calculated about her movements. She arched her carefully plucked eyebrows under her pink visor to examine her eyeliner. She backed up and, turning sideways, pulled the waist tie tighter on her sweats. That's when she saw me.

"Sophie! For goodness sake," she cried. "Are you all right?"

"I was just wondering…" but I couldn't say I was wondering the same about her because of the car. She would think I was snooping. "I just wondered if you had time to drink a cup of coffee with me. But it looks like you have plans. Playing tennis?"

"No." She laughed lightly, perhaps a tad falsely. "Not me. You caught me trying on my new look. I'll be 65 tomorrow. I was just wondering if I could pass for 60." The truth was she didn't have a bad body, but the bleached hair, pulled back into a ponytail and stuffed over the band at the back of her visor?

"Of course," I replied. "Younger, even." Like seventeen.

We live in Bridgewater Village, a condo development for retirees and snowbirds, bungalows built around a recreation center. Nearly every woman here tries going blonde at some point past 60. It seems to be a late-life rite of passage.

"I owe my skin to Angela Della Santa's grandmother,"

Deborah now said. I must have looked puzzled because she laughed and filled me in. "Fifty years ago this wrinkled old Italian crone told us girls to use olive oil to keep our beauty. Do you want that cup of coffee?"

"How about a cup of tea?"

She beckoned me into her kitchen where I could see she didn't have a coffee maker going anyway, and had to use the microwave to heat my tea. In the two minutes it took the cup to brew, I noticed she had a gin bottle on the counter and a half-filled – or half-empty – glass beside it. Perhaps sensing my wandering eyes, Deborah gently pushed it back between the breadbox and a bowl of bananas.

"I like your sporty outfit," I commented encouragingly. "It's definitely a new you." For the last couple of years, until our Home Owners Association elections last April, Deborah Conyers had been known best as "Madam Chairman" wearing tailored suits to preside over our meetings. She had seemed to aspire to the image of tough cookie, like the real estate agent in our midst who spoke kindly only to older women who were on the verge of moving to assisted living. Most people disliked Deborah's take-charge manner. Then someone spotted her at the Yacht Club with a handsome man, and reported she had looked very soft, almost kittenish. That, of course, led to speculation about who Deborah's beau might be and what they were up to. I try to keep out of these conversations, but I definitely would say she had two sides to her personality. And of course the soft one had suffered very badly.

"This is my new uniform," Deborah said, handing me the mug of tea.

"Uniform? Do you have a job at a country club?"

"No. I just mean that I took all my Madam Chairman suits back to Second Look when I finished my term on the board. I am wearing things like this instead. I guess that will leave a few mouths wide open." So she knew about the cruel talk. "From now on it will be Nike outlet style for me, because Bridgewater recreation center is going to be my only social life. I also plan to sell my Hank wardrobe." My own mouth fell open at this quirky but revealing remark. Maybe she was finally over her grieving, putting the past behind her, and moving on with her life, but she sure sounded superficial.

"What do you mean by your Hank wardrobe?" I asked.

"Hank's remarkable ability to sucker me into a so-called 'lasting' friendship was all about 'let's pretend.' The twenty million or so he inherited from an aunt was a total fiction. The status house he 'owned' wasn't his. He barely was able to keep up his club memberships. I spent a fortune on those clothes. Now I need the money."

"I hung on to them awhile after he died. But when the weather warmed up again, and my date book was still empty, I decided that …." She paused, apparently thinking how to continue. I could have finished her sentence. None of his pals were going to pick up where he had left off. Deborah never really had been part of the Yacht Club crowd. And now everyone in that crowd knew Hank had not really been one of them either. He had been a charming fraud.

"I have been wondering how you are getting along."

"Is that why you came over?"

"I saw that big, black car drive away. It scared me. I thought perhaps there was a, well, problem here."

There was a long silence, and I wasn't sure whether to jump into it with some inane observation about village security, or change the subject (My, this tea is delicious, may I have some more?). Then she spoke again, very deliberately.

"Sophie. Can I tell you something strange and perhaps wonderful that just happened? Will you promise not to tell anyone?" She didn't hesitate. Everyone knew I kept my word. Often I was called upon for advice. Not that I'm bragging. It's a double-edged sword.

I nodded.

"I'm still undecided. I have had an offer of a part time job. But it is a little mysterious. I would like to know what you think about it."

"Tell me more," I begged. I really did want to hear this one.

"That car you saw – but let me start at the beginning." She dropped to a chair, knees apart, feet flat, elbows bent, fingers tightly intertwined. "I couldn't sleep last night, so finally at about 4:30 I got up and just for kicks tried on these clothes. I went to the mirror in the hall to see how I looked. I confess I had chosen these Capri-length sweat pants to show off the better part of my legs and the v-necked tee-shirts to show just a bit of cleavage. I was thinking it covered my waistline, but" (pinching herself on two sides of her middle) "this fold of" (she couldn't bring herself to say "fat") "well, spare tire, has settled across my tummy. Just about one year ago, a month before I found him dead, Hank offered to pay for liposuction. I'm ashamed to say that this morning I was wishing I had taken him up on that. But life goes on, I said to myself, with all its imperfections. I turned sideways to see how bad it was and whether I had bulges in back. We don't usually see our backs. What the heck, I wondered. I'm 65 now, so let's have an honest assessment."

At this point I shifted in the hard wooden kitchen chair, put my mug on my paper napkin. Where was this unnecessarily detailed self-assessment headed? I began to suspect she had been drinking gin since she got out of bed.

"I lifted my shirt over my head and threw it on the floor," she continued. "I slid my pants down to my ankles. There I was in just my underpants, and right at that moment headlights *strafed* the living room walls through the front window."

"That black car?" I asked. She nodded.

"So I flipped off the sconce switches. But then it turned

into my drive! I kicked off the sweats and headed back into the hallway, feeling my way along the walls. After counting to ten and nothing more happened, I ran toward my bedroom, but the curtains were open there, too, and the car was in the driveway with its lights off. I ducked into the hall bathroom and waited. I heard a car door slam and two men with low voices talking as they moved toward the front porch. They didn't sound like anyone I knew. In another few seconds there was a rap-rap that rattled the screen door. What could I do? I found my clothes and pulled them on, then tiptoed to the front door to check through the peephole. There were two men out there on the porch, one very puffy-looking, and the other slender and suave. He had a little bit of a moustache. They both were wearing black leather jackets. At first I thought they were policemen – trouble in the neighborhood – and I put my hand on the knob. Just in time I noticed they were wearing blue jeans. I was not going to just open the door and let them in. I asked who they were.

"Who were they?"

"They said they were friends of my neighbor across the street."

"Roland Urquardt?"

"Yes. I asked them, 'What's the problem?' The suave one answered, 'He's not there. We were supposed to go fishing. We're wondering if you noticed his car back out this morning.'"

"This was at 4:30 in the morning?" I questioned, beginning to think she was spinning a shaggy dog story.

"Say five, by now. But still in the middle of the night, as far as I was concerned. The suave guy opened the screen door! Then the short one moved to try the latch! I reached for the safety chain, but was too slow in fastening it. He pushed it open so they both were looking me right in the face."

"My goodness, Deborah. You should have a panic button. That was a break-in."

"Yes. But they weren't burglars. I didn't want them there. They smelled like goats in their cheap leather, and cheap cologne. They filled the whole entryway with their big fake shoulders and yucky odors. But they just wanted information."

"So what happened next?"

"The guy who reminded me of a puff-ball glanced around the living room like Roland might be hiding behind my curtains. 'Did you see him last night?' he asked. I shook my head, but they both stepped in there and kept looking around."

"What did you do?"

"I tried not to look scared. I just said, 'I beg your pardon? Why do you think I should know where he is?' Like that." She did her best to look snooty.

"Did you ask them why they had come to you?"

"Yes. They said they saw my light on. And they claimed he had told them I was his friend."

"Are you?" This would be interesting. No one else in the neighborhood had been able to break down the barrier Roland Urquardt erected around his life. He was civil, sometimes exchanged pleasantries, but did not go out of his way.

"When I said I seldom ever saw him, the suave one got a little, well, insistent. He said, 'We know he talks to you.' I said I hadn't seen him at all this week, which was absolutely true. By then they were wandering in and out of the other rooms, opening closets in the bedrooms and the pantry in my kitchen. They seemed to be sure that I was hiding him somewhere in my house. I tried to reason with them. I asked them why he would have changed his mind about fishing without letting them know."

""That's what we wonder,' the puff-ball said."

"Why didn't you tell them to leave?" I asked her.

"I was going to. Or get out of there myself. The suave one saw me looking at the door. He stepped closer to me and I backed away until I was up against that narrow table where I pile my mail – I was stuck there. I *did* think about one of those ads for a call button necklace for old women living alone. I thought about assisted living. I nearly peed in my new pants." Deborah paused. If she was waiting for laughter from me, it was pointless. I thought about the gin again, but she seemed perfectly lucid as she continued her story. "It was getting to be daylight. I was now hoping that someone would walk into the cul de sac – like you did –see the fancy car and be a little nosy."

I could imagine other neighbors being nosy, but not brave enough to walk over to check out the situation. Bridgewater didn't have much hero material. In fact, other than Roland Urquardt, I'm Deborah's closest year-round neighbor, and most of the time I mind my own business, too.

"Puffy walked to the window and looked across at Roland's house. He accused me: 'I bet he told you not to tell anyone where he was going.' I looked him in the eye and said, 'He isn't friendly with his neighbors. No one keeps track of him.' But, Sophie, my mind was racing over the only conversation I did have with Roland recently. It raised questions in my mind about him."

"What questions?" I asked her.

"We don't usually chat when we see each other; we just wave. And I only see him when he walks his dog. But one day last week when I saw him come out in his driveway – I was really curious and a little bit puzzled about something I'd seen – I went across to talk to him." Deborah squeezed her eyes tight shut as if trying to remember word for word.

"And…?"

"Well, a couple weeks ago when I had just pulled into my garage, a delivery van pulled up to his. I wasn't sure he was home, so I thought they might come and drop a package off for him at my house. Anyway, I stayed in my car with the garage door lifted, and watched in my rear view mirror as they removed some cartons from a side door in their truck – about a dozen, all the same. They carried them around the side of Roland's garage to his back yard. Then Roland came out from his kitchen entrance and it was clear he was expecting them. I had no excuse to keep watching, but I was curious."

I thought Deborah's interest was a little excessive. Nearly everybody has something delivered sometime.

"So when I saw him that morning with his dog and went across I said, 'It looks like you're starting a new business.' He tilted his head at me and I described what I had seen."

"Did he explain?"

"No! He was rude. He said he had things to do and walked away from me."

"That wasn't exactly rude."

"Maybe not, but when I think back on it now, I believe it was those same men who came over here this morning who delivered those packages. And it didn't look like fishing equipment."

"You didn't tell me what finally happened to them this morning. How did you get them to leave?"

"The sound of another car got them excited. I hoped it was Mr. Urquardt returning. I said a little prayer, in fact. But the car circled in the cul de sac and the sound went away.

That's when they asked me to do them a favor. The puff-ball said, 'Okay, Ms. Conyers. We believe you.' They knew my name! Roland must have told them."

I noted that they hadn't told Deborah their names, and wondered why.

"So he sat down on my sofa, looked real friendly, and asked if I would like to make a little pin money. Grease Ball kept looking out the window, his hand on my clean curtain."

"The favor?"

"He explained that if I agreed to keep my eyes on that house across the street, day and night, they would pay me 250 dollars a week, 500 in advance. He said they need to know every time a person I didn't recognize comes to Urquardt's house, what car he drives, what license plate, and how long he stays. Day or night. And most important, if he unloads anything or picks anything up."

"So what did you say to Puff Ball?" I asked, now really doubting the verity of this comic sketch.

"Well, of course I said I wasn't sure how I could stay awake to keep an eye on the house night and day."

"And…?"

"He said to use an alarm clock and check every two hours. Then his partner had a better idea. They said they could install a wire in Roland's driveway that would ring a bell in my house. They would call me every couple of days to find out what I saw."

"So you agreed to do it?"

"They told me I could think it over until noon. I asked them to repeat what they wanted and wrote everything down. So I have a few hours to weigh the pros and cons."

"For 250 dollars a week you will give up your freedom to become their watchdog?"

"They said it could take months. Think about it. A steady income. A thousand a month." She showed me her notes.

"Didn't you think this was a strange request from men who claimed to be your neighbor's friends? And what about Mr. Urquardt's right to privacy?"

"But since he is so strange himself, how do I know if Roland Urquardt is a good guy or a bad guy? You see, I thought I might be helping an investigation."

"But now you think these very same men unloaded some cartons at Roland's house."

Deborah just shrugged her shoulders. She wasn't that sure what she saw. I was a little taken aback to think she wanted the money badly enough to risk getting mixed up in this funny business without being sure what it was all about. On the other hand, if she bought and sold her clothes at second hand stores, the money probably was a major attraction. Maybe this wasn't any worse than becoming a baby sitter or a home health care worker. These two characters surely didn't sound too nice to work for, but neither are some whiney children or cranky old folks.

As if reading my mind, Deborah went over to her piano and picked up a double photo frame. One picture was of Hank from the shoulders up in a white uniform of some kind. The other was the two of them seated at a table at the Crab Shack. They looked tanned and healthy, and somehow right for one another.

"He looks like a movie star."

"Yes. He was charming – but gutless. When the bank took his boat, then his car, and started foreclosure on his Cliffside house, he snuffed himself."

I nearly choked on my second cup of tea, but it wasn't that I was shocked by the news, because it wasn't fresh; it was just her way of telling it. The gossips of Bridgewater already had tittle-tattled when one of them somehow found out what had happened. He'd drugged himself to death. Some pitied Deborah. Others who thought she was opportunistic – or who were jealous of her looks – said she had it coming; they were happy to see her go down. Officially, though, no one ever said a word to her about it. In Bridgewater society, Deborah Conyers had always been outré. Even in the suits, her innate sexuality showed, which just wasn't the Bridgewater way. Will she ever learn, I wondered. Because here she was trying to look like she belonged at the center of the Bridgewater "court" society, apparently hunting for a new and younger partner.

"Why don't I just happen to be here for lunch when they come back at noon, Sweetie," I offered.

"Oh, no, Sophie. I couldn't let that happen. You see, they told me that I could not under any circumstances let anyone else know anything about this. The person or persons they were expecting might find out through the grapevine the house was being watched. That would endanger Mr. Urquardt. *Mister* Urquardt. Very respectful. I am thinking now maybe he's somebody important, and that's why he doesn't talk to us."

I nodded, but I could see she still wasn't comfortable about accepting the offer. She stood without expression for a moment as if expecting me to comment, or maybe argue. All I could do was throw up my hands.

"Your choice," I said. "I'll be here if you need me."

As I walked out of the cul de sac toward my own house on Dorado Circle I wondered how bad off she was, if she saw herself as a charity case if she did not find a way to supplement her income. She did have the condo, and it was nicer than mine. That made me feel a little better because she could always look into a reverse mortgage if things became desperate. Too bad Bridgewater Village didn't allow taking in tenants, although, truth be told, that's what some of these late life "romances" were all about.

But whatever this job offer was, it came at a bad time for Deborah Conyers to be making clear decisions. What would I have done? Well, it's a matter of how much trouble one can get into, isn't it? She didn't even know if Roland Urquardt was in danger or a gangster. And it would involve sticking close to the house. I couldn't do it.

By the time I took a shower and had a real cup of tea, I had decided it might be okay for Deborah. As long as she let the mysterious nature of their offer be of no importance – none of her business – and as long as she kept her head down and mouth shut, act like a normal woman in a grieving period, she could make enough money to make ends meet for a while, long enough to think of something else.

The teeny-tiny, niggling doubt in my mind centered on the fact that she did not know if these men actually were friends of Roland or not. They said they were, but in my mind, their behavior suggested otherwise. And, anyway, she was absolutely right: Why would Roland skip out on a fishing expedition?

I pumped the release on my ballpoint pen advertising the realtor who had sold me my little condo, and touched the point to a piece of Crane stationery that had been in its box for about fifteen years. This was too personal a chore for a computer. Besides, I could think better writing a letter the old-fashioned way. My handwriting wasn't quite as steady as it once was, and the ballpoint not as elegant as the old

Esterbrook I used to have, but it would do. The paper was a pale peach color. It looked motherly.

Dear Son, You asked me to explain why I quit my job, so here goes:

First of all, I am not going to move to be near you, so don't worry. I am quite happy here in Florida. I am healthy and still have all my marbles. (And then some.) You know I won't ever need your financial support and that I can afford to travel. But I can't blame you for asking questions. I hadn't planned on retiring from the library so soon. It was just that things changed in ways I didn't expect.

Pen up, I thought: For most of the last ten years I had my dream job, taking care of the crème de la crème of local readers – well-educated, polite – retired businessmen who were enthusiastically exploring history after years of living in the constantly shifting "real" world, and intelligent women who had their fill of country clubs and formed book discussion groups and frequently asked for my latest recommendations. I liked that. But then I inherited a bunch of hooligans from the new high school nearby that apparently has money for chain link fences, but none for books. I didn't need to say that to Robin. He might think I'm just getting old and cranky. I continued:

I started to think about it when the central administration decided to rotate the staff so that the ones working downtown near the social services offices could for a time get away from the problem of vagrants who come in to get out of the weather. I couldn't tell Robin how gross it was. These homeless men had infested the new upholstered furniture with some kind of biting insect. I just wrote: *That meant every six months or so we all would be sent to other locations in the system. It could be as boring as that tiny branch where I used to work on Costa Key, which is hardly used at all, or as frustrating as the one in a shopping center.*

Here I paused again, wondering how much he would understand. At Costa Key most of the books available – only paperbacks – are racy romance novels. There aren't many because most of them disappear into beach bags never to be seen again. The library patrons steal them instead of check them out because they don't like to admit they read them. Never mind. I wrote: *The only job I wanted was, believe it or not, downtown where the vagrants are. In spite of an occasional stench, it has its advantages. The major one is that the Dorado Bay police station is next door, and they sometimes needed my help researching some facts for a case. It has been an exciting year, and I have found a real soul mate in the chief detective, Captain Samuels.*

Now don't get the wrong idea.

I set the pen down and fell back into my late husband's leather desk chair, swiveled around to look out the window at the pond, and squinted. What else could I say about Sam? He is a distinguished-looking man about my age and, like me, tied to a job that he has come to loathe. That's really why he began to hang out in the library an hour or so each day. I have to remember that. It had nothing to do with me, at least not in the beginning. The main police station and main library are in the same complex of municipal buildings. He could have sent his assistant, but he liked getting away. Needing a trained researcher was his excuse. The Internet baffled him.

We hit it off. For one thing, both of us grew up in New York and chose to live in West Florida rather than East Florida, which is mostly New Yorkers. Here we were surrounded by people from the mysterious Midwest. Neither of us has ever been there, not even Chicago. But best of all, Sam has an admirably skeptical attitude toward just about everything we are expected to rely on: government, churches, families, and private and non-profit institutions (especially banks and hospitals). That skepticism is our bond.

"Why don't you retire?" I asked him one morning when he was in a complaining mood about the police superintendent.

"Can't afford to," he said grimly. "My ex-wife is in an expensive nursing home."

I was more than a bit shaken. I had assumed he was unattached. Still, ex-wife that he felt responsibility for, that was refreshing.

"Alzheimer's. She got it in her fifties. I'm her only relative, so to speak."

"I thought you had a son."

"Different marriage."

"Oh," I said, looking into my cup. "*Homme de couer.*"

"Do you like your work?" he asked.

"Sort of. It's changed a lot. It's all about computers."

"Hmm. Well, if you were in my shoes, you'd appreciate how fast they can get you information. And *data.*" He winced at that last bureaucratic term.

"I know. But the recent library graduates are the anointed 'information' experts," I said. "They don't give me much time at the terminals. When you come in and ask for me in particular, that really boosts my stock."

"Is there something you'd rather be doing?"

"What *you* do sounds interesting to me. Catching the bad guys."

"Ha! I don't always."

"What's the problem?"

"There are too many. And they're different these days. They could look like you or me."

"Tell me about an unsolved crime," I then demanded, I thought sweetly. I am not known for feminine cunning, but it got him talking and me thinking.

You know, son, I'm a pretty good problem-solver when it comes to helping people who get themselves into difficult situations. (Even though you are sometimes embarrassed and call me a buttinski.) *Sam encourages me to put those talents to use for the public good when he asks for my help with a research question. He might want to know more about a clothing manufacturer, or how long ago a certain metal was first made. He asks me to look up family names on genealogical charts.*

At some point my fascination went beyond that. On that break I mentioned, seated side by side on a bench in the rose memorial garden between the library and the police station, I got Sam talking about some of his unsolved cases. He couldn't tell me much, no name, just the circumstances. I mulled over the facts until the next time we met, drawing on my vast experience with real people but also fiction (life imitates art, was my premise at the time). He listened. Then I would do a little more research and come up with "new avenues to pursue." While I admit these were often highly imaginative routes to explore, and some were dead ends, my suggestions sometimes did trigger more original thinking in the old workhorse. But all I wrote to my son was this:

When Captain Samuels became convinced that it actually gave a librarian pleasure to look things up in the reference department, and even pour through old newspapers on microfilm, he began to give me more assignments, little facts he was chasing. Sam and I made an effective team. I saved him time. He doesn't have much help in his department, and doesn't trust what help he has to be thorough. There are many questions that the World Wide Web cannot answer without many hours wasted being bounced from pillar to post in the maze of interconnectivity. They would give up too easily. I know the shortcuts. That is the nature of a librarian's job.

But, as I said, personnel policy changed, and I had to quit. I didn't know what was going to fill my time next, but my sense was it would turn out all right if I could continue to work for Sam.

"I'm retiring from librarianship," I told the police detective one day when we had taken our customary places on the long bench sheltered from any of our colleagues by the wall of wax myrtle between our buildings. What I had hoped would happen did happen: Sam's face fell. He had come to rely on me.

"I don't get it, Sophie," he said, "I thought you were enjoying yourself."

"I am, with you. It's the library board. They've decided to go back to the old rotation. The director wants me back on Costa Key, where life's a beach. It's like being put out to pasture."

"But what will you do?"

By now Sam knew that I had had my fill of bridge, golf, and anything merely social. I wasn't sure that he understood I need a serious purpose. I hoped he would say he couldn't get along without me. But he didn't. So I made a suggestion.

I offered to continue to help the captain when he needed me, I wrote. I was probing, of course. I reminded him that I have my own computer. His reaction was not quite what I'd hoped. Instead of thanking me and immediately suggesting an assignment, he told me that the library was a public place with a secure system and people to maintain it. My personal computer was not safe. He said I had no idea how brutal the underworld in Florida really was. Although I was quick to score on domestic violence, he admitted, in Florida "family" also meant something much bigger. There were things he couldn't tell me, he said. If he did, I might meddle and soon I'd be in over my head. The word "meddle" really got to me, but when I thought about it later I decided that what he really feared was changing our relationship. When I was just a librarian, a public servant, he never had to tell me anything about the big picture his office was working on, just bits and pieces. If he consulted me outside of a library, I would be a crime specialist. As a consultant, I could ask probing questions. His reluctance worried me, but one day I handed in my resignation and asked Sam to celebrate with me over our last cup of coffee. That is, the last cup in the library garden.

"I've thought about it," I said as dryly as I could manage, "and I do want to continue helping you." Sam opened his mouth to say something, stopped, and then clamped his lips together as if controlling a thought. Maybe he was wondering if I expected to be paid. Since I didn't need "pin money" I quickly added, "I'll be a volunteer, of course." I once had a neighbor who worked with the Sheriff's Department, even went out on calls with the Deputy. I couldn't imagine Sam letting me tag along, so I added, "I'll work at home and be on call. I'll be anonymous." He sighed. That was all.

We had been sitting over empty cups for almost half an hour. It was now 10:45. My colleagues had arranged a goodbye party for 2:30 and then I'd clean up my workspace and leave. I looked at Sam, still silent, eyes wandering over the line of other civil servants waiting to give their orders at the counter. Some were on late morning breaks, others already ordering lunch. Did I really want to wait for a firm reply?

"I guess I'd better get back." I stood, keeping my eyes on the chair as I pushed it in neatly. One of my pet peeves is when people – like my dear late husband – don't push their chairs in at the table when they are finished eating.

"Won't they miss you?" Sam asked softly as I secured my bag on my shoulder. That's as far as he could go toward saying *he* would miss me. That would have hurt except that it left the door open for our future collaboration.

"Never. I'm old guard, someone to be tolerated for the duration," I said, cackling like a wise old crone. "They think they know everything – or that the computer does. And everyone knows a ten-year-old is swifter with the new technology than someone my age. But I'm no dummy. I've been around longer."

He called me at home early the next morning. It wasn't much of a challenge. He needed some help tracing the origins of the family that owned a liquor store.

I have to admit, Robin, I wrote, *that until the police work came my way, I was getting quite depressed. After all, I had been a career woman for less than twenty years. It seemed as if I had just started to hit my stride when the library directors pulled the rug out from under me with the new rotation policy. I didn't want to stop working. You know I have the intelligence. Your grandmother's genes, of course. I can't sit and watch the world go by any more than she could when your grandfather died. She took over the reins and made his little company into a contender. That's what paid for Yale and Columbia and Vassar. You and your cousins should remember that.*

Son, please believe me when I tell you it wasn't an overnight decision. For some time I'd been trying to work out what I could do that would give me more satisfaction, and now I know I have found my niche as a detective's research assistant. I'll let you know how it goes. But please trust me. Your doubts have really hurt my feelings.

When I'd first told Robin, months ago, over the phone, that I was thinking about quitting my job, he had been quite unreasonable. He told me I would be miserable after a week, reminded me that there were no signs of my ever having a grandchild to brighten my days – as if that's all a woman ever needed. He even suggested I take a vacation and think about it a little more before handing in my resignation. My initial reaction to his advice was more emotional than I like to admit. I was cruel. I told him I suspected he was only worried about himself, worried that I might start being a pest, or that I would start living it up and spend his entire inheritance.

Since then we had not engaged in a meaningful conversation. I was frankly demoralized that he hadn't encouraged me. I didn't call him to apologize and he didn't call me to apologize. And when two weeks had passed he phoned one night to let me know he had been assigned to a project in Egypt for six months. I was "all business" (his words thrown back at me later), although my heart ached. "Sounds like a great opportunity," was about what I said. I hardly remember. A few miserable days went by and then, when he knew I would be at work, he left a message saying he was "deeply sorry about the way we had left our conversation," but could I please explain it all again, especially who Sam was, and what I would be doing for him. And he asked if he could come and spend a weekend with me before he left for Egypt so we could talk face to face.

I was happy to hear him apologize, but didn't want him to come to visit me now and maybe discourage Sam from asking for my help. So, the letter.

After writing two more paragraphs sketching my plan, telling him how busy I was, and giving my only child some reassurances about his inheritance, I read the letter to myself out loud – a very good thing to do, I had learned years before – and signed it, adding "x's" and "o's," a foolish custom I'd kept up since he was old enough to go to camp. I addressed the matching Crane envelope, its flap lined with gold paper, thinking it would be the last time I'd use that address for a while. How would I reach him in Egypt? I scrawled the question as a "P.S." and folded the letter around a photograph of the two of us standing beside our car. Robin was aged 10 and going away to camp; I was 48 and trying not to shed a tear. No, I told myself. I don't want to play dirty and pull heartstrings. Let him think of me as the wise, old, independent-minded woman I am. I took the picture out, inserted the letter alone, sealed the envelope, and put a stamp on it. I stuck it in my purse that was waiting on the rattan chair beside the desk.

I stood up, emotionally wrung out, stretched, and stood quietly looking out the picture window that faces the pond. I mentally reviewed my accomplishments in the few months since Sam's offer saved me from complete retirement. I had created discipline for myself, starting each day as soon as it was light with a brisk walk twice around the circle of condos that backed onto the pond. I always aimed to finish before anyone else was out, thereby avoiding mundane conversations before I'd had my coffee and morning news. I'd then make my bed – always made my bed. It's a real sign of aging not to. The next hour was devoted to paying bills, if I had them. Otherwise, I would simply make notes from the *Wall Street Journal* for my next meeting with Curtis Roberts. It was wise to let your stockbroker know you keep up with market developments.

Starting at nine, I work at my computer on whatever tasks Sam has given me that week. On nice days I might have a ten-lap swim at the community pool. Yes, ten. If you slack off you're in trouble. Back home, I stick my little bit of laundry in the washing machine. I nibble on raw carrots and have instant soup in a cup, fold my clean laundry and put it away. No later than two I go back to the computer, and often find myself over-researching the topic. That's the dark side of the Internet. I am aware of the dangers of amassing trivia. That's something I'm working on, trusting and then focusing my own instincts.

Before the afternoon is gone, I will force myself out of the house, often to see a friend who is recuperating from surgery, as frequently there is one of those; and other times I might have a detail that requires a trip to the library downtown. I go in with my head bowed to avoid contact with my former colleagues. If they spot me I head for the shelves labeled "Fiction." They don't have to know what I am doing.

Home at five or six, depending on whether or not I stop for groceries, I sit in the Florida room to read the local paper. That takes ten minutes, as long as I avoid the obituaries. Once a week, another half hour is taken up with phone calls to my two sisters, both older than I am. For reasons I cannot explain, I have not yet told them that I no longer work at the library. That's why I wait until evening to call, as before. If they ask about the library, I manage (so far) to steer conversation back to what they have been doing. As they are in their seventies that amounts to trips to doctors, visits from dutiful children, and gardening (in one case) and bridge games (the other). Or books. We all are avid readers of current fiction and biographies – not the cheap stuff, like Princess Diana, but books by real historians. The three of us were the brightest girls in our schools, celebrated by teachers and dubbed by our peers as "the owls." We had identical round-rimmed glasses provided by a government home health nurse, and, to our shame, unfashionable, faded, hand-me-down clothes. Need I mention we had no boyfriends. Our mother always said that our marriages were miracles, even more so since she had given up religion and praying when our father left us. Rita married young and stayed married until she nagged Bernard into his grave. Minnie worked at the telephone company until she married a widower who had two young daughters. I waited until I was 35. I feel lucky to have had one son. Most of the time.

I like my life. Sam keeps our contacts to phone calls except for once weekly appointments on Fridays for dinner. He picks me up at my house where we have a drink and go over the facts of a case. I tell him what I have found, hand over documents, etc. Then we head for a restaurant for a light meal. Over coffee or dessert he tells me what he still needs. Once it was a name previously used by a suspect, another time a list of places someone resided. Once it was a model of car that no longer was made. Another time, in a relationship-defining moment, he asked if I could find a recipe for Brunswick Stew.

"What does Brunswick Stew have to do with the case?" I was fascinated.

"It doesn't. I just got a hankering for it. I had some when I went up to Georgia to see my buddy." Fortunately, during this conversation we were having an after-dinner drink on my back patio, his fourth, so I didn't have to make a disturbance in public. I put him straight: I am not interested in being his *personal* assistant. I had agreed only to give technical assistance in a crime investigation – *as a professional researcher*! Since then he has asked me to do only serious work.

I strolled to the corner postbox to mail my letter to Robin. I don't like to give the mailman more to carry than he already has, and I enjoy the walk. I am determined to keep walking. I am the kind of person who parks at the far end of the parking lot when I go to the supermarket or drugstore. But I don't do it aerobically. I am not overweight. If anything, I could gain a few pounds. When we lived on the island, a chubby neighbor told me, in the middle of a cocktail party, that she could tell who in our crowd had a deprived childhood. That was just about everyone but her. We are the pre-Atkins generation. We don't need anyone who sits typing in a book-lined study on a California golf course to tell us how not to look over-fed. Our children – well, their story is quite different. Robin's girlfriends spend half their waking hours with their personal trainers.

Walking home from the mailbox, I enjoyed the sunshine

and breeze too much to go right back to the computer. I got my toughest gardening gloves and my pruning clippers from the shelf in the carport and made my way to the back of my house. These condos are detached. We have maybe twenty feet between our outer walls. Some people don't have plants, especially if their spaces are always in the shade, or if they rarely use these homes. I can't live without a few. Perhaps it's because of my mother and her vegetable garden, our main income for several years. I can't say I ever grew vegetables after we moved to New Jersey, and I only kept house plants when Robin's father and I moved to Florida. I was too busy with raising Robin in the one instance, and with golf and cocktail parties in the other. But here in Bridgewater Village I enjoy the hibiscus and a few rose bushes I inherited from the previous owners.

On my knees, nipping and shaping the plants that mark the line between my backyard and the common grounds that rim the pond, out of the corner of my left eye, I saw something moving at the edge of the water, beyond the irises. I thought it might be an exotic bird. Standing up I could see it was a piece of colorful fabric, like maybe somebody lost a scarf and it blew down there. I walked a few steps in that direction, down the sloping lawn. Odd. It looked like a necktie floating there, occasionally waving at me, beckoning me to come over and have a closer look. I couldn't resist, though when I got as far as the water irises, my feet soaking wet from the sprinklers, I decided to go back to my house to get the binoculars Robin gave me when he decided I should take up bird-watching. I grabbed them off the window ledge in the Florida room and returned to the spot where, with some difficulty focusing the device, I could see it was definitely a scarf or necktie. Magnified, it was an even stranger sight. I laughed at first, at its undulation on the surface of the brownish-green water like a small and colorful sea monster. But when I looked beyond the tie I felt my throat tighten. I recognized the face of our mysterious neighbor whose house Deborah was asked to watch. Roland Urquardt stared wide-eyed under that garish necktie. Fortunately, I don't panic. The first thing I did was go into the kitchen to call 911. The second thing I did was to grab my steno notebook and ball point pen. Then I went back outside, staying at the rim of my patio, about forty feet from the water's edge.

It seemed a long time that I stood there taking it all in. With the binoculars, I could see that the whole body was visible just under the surface, jammed into the weeds at the edge of the oval water feature that had been dug out of the middle of the sixteen acres that make up the Bridgewater Village neighborhood. They aren't in fact weeds, but rather flowers strategically planted to hide the infrastructure around the pond – the concrete curbs, the pumps, the screens that keep debris away from the overflow. The irises were inconspicuous in bloom, but some other species growing profusely at the pond's edge had a wide crown of stringy leaves hanging all around the stem, suggesting a crowd of torn umbrellas. Just below my lawn, many of these stalks were bent as though they had been burdened with the weight of a body thrown in on top of them.

I looked through the binoculars again. This isn't easy with trifocals. It's hard enough to find the spot you're looking for, but then you have to compensate by making adjustments, and repeat the process any time you move to another object. I couldn't find Roland's feet. I decided it wasn't my eyesight, but that they must be dangling further below the waterline. Presumably he was wearing heavy shoes. Or – if this was like a gangster movie – his feet would be encased in cement blocks. I wanted something to laugh about. This was getting serious. This was real. I concentrated on the observable. He had on a brown suit coat, but it was unbuttoned and flailing at his sides. The lining was darker brown. The shirt he wore was checked with thin dark lines. Against it, the green, red and black tie stood out boldly, wide, a banner. The pattern looked kind of Japanese, like a painted kimono. It was not a tie I would have chosen for that brown suit, or for any occasion, and it didn't look like Roland Urquardt's style, either, from what I'd seen of him alive.

I couldn't understand why his body rocked from side to side until finally I deduced that it was stuck over the spot where the pond is replenished each day with gray water.

The pump, painted purple to distinguish its use was clearly visible.

There was no chance of getting much closer without possibly interfering with the crime scene. I was contemplating the risk when I heard cars screeching to a halt in front of my house. I trudged up the bank to meet the emergency personnel in their orange vests and then led them down the sloping lawn to the strap-like, knee-high plants. A few other residents whose back doors faced the pond now came over this way to see what was going on. A couple of officers went over to calm them and urge them to go inside. Three of their colleagues were struggling to put up the yellow caution tape to secure the area leading to the water's edge. As soon as the rescue team pulled the body up onto the slope of lawn, and saw the bashed-in crown of the victim's skull, the yellow tape went up around the entire pond and commons area, fencing out the twenty-two identical, pale green stucco condo units that formed a ring around it. Now there were many more disaster-hungry Bridgewater residents crowding the pond-facing patios. Some of them had binoculars, too. Within minutes, two competing TV crews rolled into the street and reporters and cameramen came rushing on foot between the condos.

But where were the investigators?

"Isn't Detective Samuels coming?" I asked a policeman checking their credentials.

"He's in Orlando. Someone else will be along shortly." Then I remembered Sam had mentioned a meeting he was going to today. He said he might get back too late for our usual *tête a tête*. It was just as well. I needed time to think. Already I began to see how I could use this tragedy – oh Lord, forgive me – to my advantage.

Two nearly expressionless investigative officers in dark blue uniforms, one male, one female, sat with me in the Florida room to hear my story. I told them what I had seen and approximately when. I filled them in with what I knew about my lone wolf neighbor, not much more than what I had observed from my patio: his occasional appearance on the path that led around the pond, to fish from one of little wooden docks, usually the one closest to my house. Yes, we had talked a few times, but very briefly. He'd once shown me what new bait he was trying out. Actually, now that I thought about it, he had told me he had been a lifelong fisherman.

They asked me if I knew if he fished at sea. I didn't. They asked how long he'd been here.

"I only met him a couple of years ago, soon after I moved in," I said. "But he told me he'd been coming down to Dorado Bay since before it was incorporated – in the early 1940s, when he was about ten. His grandfather owned a winter home here." Dorado Bay was then a village in the remotest part of the west Florida coast, so unlike the social Mecca that attracted people to Florida's east coast cities. Roland had no relatives here now, as far as I knew.

"Was he married?" the female, Lieutenant Nancy Peterman, asked.

"I don't know. I assumed he lived alone here. He had a sister in New York. He mentioned that when he found out I was a librarian. She was a librarian, too, he said. That's all he ever told me about his family." In fact, we had this conversation the one time he happened to come into the library downtown when I was on the desk. I was surprised to see him there. He certainly wasn't one of our regulars. I wondered if that was relevant, but decided not to tell them. Selfish, in a way. I didn't want them to think of me as "the librarian."

"Did he mention his own profession?" This was from the male, who said he was Lieutenant Blaine Hobson.

"He told me he had been a practicing attorney until he moved here permanently, in 1987. I don't know if he meant Bridgewater Village; I would guess that's when he came back to Dorado Bay," I clarified. I had thought at the time, because his answers were so brief, that something he didn't want to talk about might have happened. He was young to have retired from law practice. Think of all the money he was giving up! It was probably a death, or, more likely, divorce. I didn't pass that along to the investigators. I would seem to be a gossip. That reminded me of Deborah. Should I tell these officers about her visitors and their request? But I had promised her I would not tell anyone. Still, the circumstances had changed. I shilly-shallied.

"Maybe some of my neighbors saw or heard something. Everyone who lives around the pond looks out now and again during the day. Lots of herons and other birds come here." They thanked me and said they would start to make the rounds. In fact, they stood by their vehicles for the next ten minutes making mobile phone calls and finally set off in opposite directions, going door to door, just like encyclopedia salesmen used to do back in New Jersey when Robin was young. Or political campaign workers asking for support.

I then hot-footed it over to Deborah's to let her know what had happened before the officers got to her cul de sac. Who knows what they would make of her story about the men in black jackets, especially if, in spite of her promise, she told them they had asked her to watch Roland's house. She needed some advice.

Now Deborah isn't really what I could call a good friend, not even the kind of person I would invite to lunch. I don't know why I say that. I'm not a snob. But I don't know much about her and she's a little embarrassing these days, all that bleach and too much gin. But I felt she was treated unfairly by the Bridgewater "in" crowd. In my own mind, I had decided she must have had some kind of responsible career to be able to preside over the HOA board like she did. No matter that nobody else wanted to do it. She stayed on track. Now I saw things a little differently, another facet, you might call it. If what she said this morning was true, that she was worried about money, she must not have saved up for retirement. Maybe she hadn't worked after all. Some women our age have made a career of volunteer activity. That could have been her case. Maybe her husband left her. Maybe he was a drunk. Or maybe he got sick and they spent all their savings on his care. There probably was no pension from him. My concern for her now was a little like the feeling I get when I see the runt of the litter, a puppy with a bent tail or differently-colored eyes. No one wanted her. She was defenseless. I had to go to her and at least make sure she wasn't going to get tangled up in a murder.

She answered the door wearing the same outfit she had been trying on at 5 a.m. But no makeup. This wasn't the Deborah I knew.

"Did they come back?" I asked anxiously.

"No, they didn't." I breathed a sigh of relief until she added, "But I got two phone calls." She went into the kitchen and I followed.

"After you left, I thought about the money they gave me already. They just left it there on the hall table. I hadn't done anything to deserve it. I put it in my purse and then took it out again. Then I tucked it into an envelope thinking I'd give it back when they returned. Then I blended a banana into some orange juice and protein powder. Hank used to buy me that stuff by the case. And I realized I wasn't going to have many more of those on my income. I found it hard to swallow." She looked at me mournfully and hadn't even realized her pun.

"And the phone calls?"

"I was restless. Then I got a brainstorm. I decided to call Roland Urquardt's house. Maybe there was a clue to his whereabouts on the answering service. But the phone rang and rang and rang. There was no answering machine. He had always seemed a little, you know…"

"Evasive?"

"Yes, evasive about his comings and goings. I realized I had been pretty stupid. If there was something going on under the table, so to speak, I didn't want to be involved."

"Did you think about calling the police?"

"No. Because of what I started to tell you about the two phone calls to me." Deborah explained that the calls had come within minutes of one another between eleven and noon. Different voices but similar conversations. They seemed meant to be intimidating but they were completely devoid of information. They warned Deborah to follow the directions she would get later, but they didn't tell her anything new. They said nothing about the money. The first time she mostly just listened, but said "uh huh" and "okay" enough to let the caller know she understood.

"It was not one of the men who came here," Deborah insisted. "This caller sounded kind of twangy. He just told me to be watching for a message, a sign of something I was to do. I supposed it was about the arrangement, but he didn't mention Roland by name."

"What else did you notice about his speech? Did he talk fast or slow?" I asked her.

"In between, I guess. It didn't occur to me that it was odd. But some words had an 'aitch' on the end. They were breathy. Like 'huh.' I guess he sounded like a prize fighter." She admitted she hardly could pay attention. Her teeth were chattering, she was so cold with fear, and the excitement made her feel like she had to get to the bathroom. She thought he said something like, "Keep your eyes and ears open, because *somethinkhuh*' will surprise you."

"Some*thinkhuh*?"

"Yeah. That was odd."

"It sounds to me like he had a cold," I suggested. Not much of a clue. "Well, had you made up your mind?" I demanded to know. "And what about the other call? Who was that?"

"I was still trying to decide whether or not to agree to be the house-watcher when the other call came about ten minutes later. I completely lost it. I just yelled, 'Is this about the job or not?' He did not answer the question. I repeated it. There was no response to that, either, just a reminder to stay alert. I asked: 'How will I know what to do?'"

"'You'll know, don't worry,' was all he said and then he hung up."

"I suppose they just wanted to know that you were there watching. What did this one sound like?" I asked her.

"His voice was *very* deep, slow, a little spooky, like he was deliberately trying to sound weird. But it still wasn't like one of the men who visited."

"Could the callers have been the same men who came to see you this morning, disguising their voices?"

Deborah shrugged. She had a tissue balled up in her palm, the box on the table, so I guessed she had been crying.

"If they were the ones, or if they are all working together, then they plan some other form of communication, I gather. Well, Deborah, I have very bad news, and it might actually be the message, or sign, they told you to be watching for." Her eyes grew wide and wider as I related the events of the afternoon.

"Omigod. I can't believe it! I can't take something so threatening, so stressful, happening to me so soon after ...." She started, self-pityingly. Her reaction disappointed me. No sympathy expressed concerning the death of a neighbor, even if he was not a good friend. It was all about her. I ignored it as best I could and focused on the real victim.

"Do you think Roland was in danger? Why hadn't he come home the last few days?" Deborah shook her head. She didn't have a clue. I gathered she had not even wondered about it. By then I was more than a little disgusted.

"The police are going to ask you these questions, Deborah. They are talking to everyone on Dorado Circle who might have seen something going on at the pond. I am sure they will come here, too, because you are his closest neighbor. If you aren't ready to talk about this, I suggest you take a walk and come back after you've had a good think." Then I had a think. I added, "You certainly have to tell them that two men came here early this morning looking for your neighbor. That much *you absolutely must* tell them." I didn't have to add the rest of my advice, that she could skip the part about their offer, at least for now. Because they hadn't come back and she hadn't really said yes.

Back in my own living room, I sat by my front window and watched events unfold. One officer was warning drivers away from this end of Dorado Circle. Then, just as the door-to-door inquiry officers were headed back in this direction, I spotted Deborah coming out of her alley into Dorado Circle, turning away from us, going toward the main thoroughfare where there's a bus stop and supermarket. She had her head down, ponytail up, and was shifting from one side of the street to the other. For 65, she was going pretty fast.

That's when I made my phone call to Sam's office. It

was still too early for him to have returned, so I dictated my message to Sergeant Purcell, his new assistant. "Meet me here when you get back. I have something special for your dinner." I was appealing to my detective friend's baser instinct – hunger. If it sounded a little naughty to the younger policeman, so be it.

For once I felt I had the upper hand. I was here, first on the scene of a murder. On my own turf. Sam would barely have any information yet. But would he believe me? I wished I had a Madam Chairman outfit to wear for this occasion. But probably more important was the food, so I made a short list: T-bones, baking potatoes, makings for chef salad, bourbon, red wine. Lots of wine. For him, not me. I had to keep a clear head. I'd put cranberry juice in my glass. Then I went to my bedroom closet and took out the light blue silk slacks and blouse outfit that is feminine, but not in an obvious way. I would even roll up the sleeves to look more businesslike. My left brain told me that I shouldn't worry about what to wear. My right brain was suggesting I should meet Sam this time with a visual statement: No more mousy librarian.

Ah! But there was something else. It was only quarter to four. The library was open until five-thirty.

I parked my out-of-date but beautiful emerald Olds in front of the library where there were lots of empty meters on a Friday afternoon. I was rather overdressed for a typical library patron, and so I waited in the foyer reading notices until my former colleagues were busy with other people. Then I headed straight for the antiquated wooden card catalog shoved against the back wall of the reference room. Most people would never think to use it, but there are things there that never made it to the restrictive code of the electronic system. Those old-time librarians sometimes poured their wizened little journalistic hearts out in the listings, especially on topics in the vertical files, memorabilia of sorts. I should explain that our little library system was once responsible for the local history collection, and some of it remained with us when the Dorado Bay Historical Society was formed, mainly to exhibit their many donated artifacts. The two boards of directors still fight over certain holdings, especially family histories. We librarians argue that they should stay where the genealogical society has set up their resources, at our downtown main library.

The card catalog yielded nothing on Roland Urquardt. He apparently had kept a low profile since he arrived in 1987. It did, however, contain a card that cited a newspaper article from 1963 about someone by the name of *Rudolph* Urquardt, "Dorado Bay winter resident, art patron and donor to the art museum."

I went to the end row of drawers, close to the door leading back to the stacks where patrons these days were not allowed. To the right of that door was a short hallway leading to the restrooms. In front of both openings was a book jacket display board, which made it easier to slip unnoticed to the forbidden part of the building. I located the actual newspaper, not the microfiche, which would have required sitting in the open reference area where I would be noticed. I took the paper over to a corner of the stacks where there was a small table set up for the library school interns to use when they worked here.

The Saturday edition was slim, eight pages in all, and the article was on page two. It was mainly a photograph of a man handing another man an envelope with an inset photo of a big house. The man identified as Rudolph Urquardt looked to be in his fifties. That was way too young to be Roland's grandfather, certainly. It could possibly be his father, but Roland hadn't mentioned him. Still, everyone has one somewhere. The caption read: "Rudolph Urquardt (left) has donated $250,000 for the maintenance of a small but valuable collection of several European paintings his family gave to the Dorado Bay Art Gallery last year." The article announced that he was "adding a gallery to his family mansion, built in 1922 (see inset), to house his growing collection of Modern Art." It didn't say whether or not his new gallery would be open to the public. More disappointing, there was no mention of any other family member. No wife, no son. No grandson. No progenitor who built the house in 1922, when he would have been an infant. The house was grand, but not what I would call pretty. I decided Rudolph Urquardt must have been a bachelor, maybe Roland's uncle, or cousin.

There was more research ahead, but the librarians were preparing to close the place up, so I got out before any of them saw me. It was then that I thought about Millie, the owner of the dress shop on the corner across from the library. She might know something about the Urquardt family. She catered to society matrons and, although she pretended to be discreet, could be persuaded to leak juicy stories about people she "would not dare name," but hinted at, as if you knew them, too. I didn't, but I could work on it. It was too late today, but maybe tomorrow I'd pay her a call.

I stopped at the supermarket for the dinner fixings including two bottles of Sam's favorite cabernet and some 101-proof Wild Turkey to my cart. By the time I got back to Bridgewater Village, except for the yellow tape, my street now looked normal, with the other ten-year-old Oldsmobiles, Buicks and Cadillacs parked in the driveways, and just two official, lime green vehicles on the curb.

By seven I was almost ready, having just broken the lettuce leaves over the freshly made French dressing. Before I placed the new bottle of bourbon on the bar end of the kitchen counter, I poured the top few ounces into a jar with a lid and stuck it in the cupboard. This reduced the chances that Sam would be observant enough to see I had bought it to please him.

I settled down in the Florida room with my binoculars. Only three officers in slickers had been left behind in the fading light to continue poking around in the pond. This made me think they didn't consider it a high profile crime. One man was using a steel pole to probe the area where the body had been found, and one was jotting notes on a spiral bound flip tablet. The third, examining the grassy edge of the pond, looked like a woman, though it was hard to tell, the short yellow coats were so stiff. It was something about the way the collar was pulled up. I really liked the idea that one of them might be female.

As I followed their movements, I silently thanked Robin for having purchased such excellent bird-watching equipment, though at the time I had scolded him for spending too much. *"You want to see if the bird is wearing a leg band, Mother, and what the numbers are."* I had hardly ever used them, until today. When Sam rolled into my drive I was studying the heavy sports watch on one policeman's wrist, and almost could read the digits flashing orange.

Sam didn't bother to ring the doorbell. He banged on the screen door at my carport entrance and marched right in. He looked furious.

"Why didn't you tell me what was going on?"

"You weren't in town to tell." That was a subtle reminder that he had never offered to give me the number of his mobile phone.

"You could have left a more detailed message."

"Not with Sgt. Purcell." I smiled.

"But he made it sound like it was just the usual…"

"Surely you don't want your fledgling assistant to know you talk to me about your cases," I interrupted, as though it were understood. Sam glowered and accepted his Turkey on the rocks. He had learned about the body when Purcell called him at the police college in Orlando where he had been asked to stay after the meeting to talk to some potential recruits. The location of the crime hadn't registered, so preoccupied was he with his preparation. He grumbled on about "too much to do" as if having to justify why he didn't remember the name Bridgewater Pond, which was in his consultant's backyard.

"When did you get my message?" I asked.

"I saw Purcell's sticky note on my computer screen, but I didn't read it right away. I had to make a budget decision first. An interactive database would be a hell of a revolution. With computers crunching numbers it's getting a little harder for cities to automatically blame low-income neighborhoods for the heat wave spikes in shootings. Somehow, a bludgeoning in an upscale neighborhood didn't seem so important. I figured it was either a robbery or a domestic crime."

"Wife gone berserk?" I suggested. He glared at me ever more fiercely. He has a great glaring ability, I must say. I like to provoke him sometimes, tease it out. He glares; I win.

I handed him a platter holding two raw steaks trimmed of fat and brushed with oil and garlic. Sam took it awkwardly, hugging it to his body while hanging tightly onto his drink by the other hand as if he expected me to take it away from him. He nodded at the back door. I pushed it open and saw him out, returning to the sink chuckling inwardly at his gruffness. How he hated losing control.

"Well, I might have recognized the M.O.," he yelled from the yard. I went out with my faux bourbon – iced tea – and a dish of olives He still seemed annoyed, so I just lifted my shoulders in a shrug as if to say I could not have done anything more than allow events to unfold in his department's own bungling hands. I went back to the house to set the table and watched him through the patio doors. He got on his mobile phone as he was slapping the steaks around. The smoke from the grill seemed to be coming from his ears. He was nonetheless a handsome man, all the more attractive to women because he looked a little sad.

After we had finished eating inside, I carried a candle lantern to the low table between my two lawn chairs, and we sat down facing the pond. It was going to be hard to get Sam into a reflective state of mind. He was all too aware of the yellow tape fluttering in the slight breeze. Thankfully, the investigators had finished before dark, so there were no spotlights, and it almost seemed like any other June evening, with everyone indoors watching television and frogs and crickets and cicadas filling the gap of silence with evidence that the humans were outnumbered. It was nice, and I almost wished we didn't have to talk business.

Sam hadn't yet relaxed by the time I brought him his second drink, but he looked my outfit up and down with a thoughtful expression, and then he pulled out the wrought iron chair for me when it was time to sit down at the patio table. I praised his perfectly done steaks profusely. We had melon slices with port for dessert, and now we were sipping a small amount of port on ice, but I was just touching my lips to it. I asked him about his talk and the week's political gossip – the mayor's divorce – before I switched to the more compelling subject.

"What do you think has happened here, Sam?"

"Hell, I don't know," he answered. "I never heard of this guy before. You say he's been around since 1987?"

"That's what I gather. At least, he said that's when he moved permanently to Dorado Bay. He told me that he used to visit his grandfather here." I tugged my sweater closer around my shoulders as the breeze picked up a little and Sam asked if I wanted to go inside. "Oh, no. This is nice."

The water stirred where a fish jumped up to catch a hovering darner. Sam didn't say anything more about Urquardt's death, but I could tell he was thinking about it. I didn't want him to know how eager I was to talk about it. I thought I had better not tell him I'd already been to the library to look up the family name. I continued my side of the conversation rather vaguely.

"He didn't say if the grandfather was an Urquardt, too. It might have been on his mother's side. Do you know of any other Urquardts living in Dorado Bay?" I asked.

"Nope." He shrugged, staring out into the darkness. "But I suppose you could find out easy enough."

"I could look it up," I said. He didn't reply, so I pushed ahead: "You know, Sam – this situation is something I might be able to lend insight to, and not just because he was my neighbor." Sam looked at the backs of his hands, where the season's first no-see-ums landed. I paused long enough to see if I had aroused his curiosity. When he looked up he looked directly into my eyes. I think he knew I knew I was stepping out to the very edge of a precipice. I blurted, "I want to explain how I would interview people if I were seriously on this case."

He looked up at the sky and yawned, and folded his arms behind his head.

"We haven't even got the autopsy report. Or Crimes Scene's."

Was there a sneer in his response? Or was it defense? Maybe he was taken aback by my self-promotion, having grown used to my respectful deference in our conversations about what he called "the crime-busting business," *his* work. I had been a good pupil over these last several months – but it was his whole life.

"We have plenty of people who can finish interviews on this case. There may be some follow-up you can help with," he conceded. He slapped a bug away and then pushed his hands against the chair arms, to get up to go. I stopped him with my hand on his wrist.

"I'd like a real assignment for a change,"

"Real?"

"Why not let me loose on Roland Urquardt's background. Not just for you, but – you know – for the *official* investigation."

"Pardon me? You'd like to *officially* work for DBPD? "

"Yes." I squinted down at the pond, heart pounding, and then convinced myself he deserved a response that was mean-spirited. "Paid." I peeked sideways at his frown, his pursed lips, his hunched shoulders, beyond which the pond water shimmered with the borrowed light of arc lamps shining between condos. I expected a lecture, but his expression softened.

"Sophie, you know I can't do that. We barely pay our new officers a living wage. We don't waste money on consultants."

"Yes, you do. I read about it in the paper." I reminded

him of the exposé of the former chief who had called in a chum from Dallas – retired cop – to lead an investigation of the newspaper reporter who was accused of killing an editor.

"'Former' says it all. That was two years ago." One reason Sam disliked his job so much these days was that the new chief who replaced the one accused of cronyism was intimidated by what had happened and did everything by the book. Boring. Or borrrinnnggg, as Sam would have said out loud, mimicking the young.

"That's why we don't have consultants any more. Anyway, you're not a cop. You're a librarian. What can you do?" Sarcasm. As I reached up to touch my pearls to keep from losing my cool, he raised both his hands palm up as if he meant it as a joke, and continued, "Besides, this looks like an easy case, probably something to do with robbing the guy's home safe."

"Why on earth do you think that?"

"Dexter said it looked like his place had been ransacked."

"Looked?"

"Well, it was pretty torn up. Unless the guy was a slob, somebody was there looking for something. We'll know more tomorrow."

He said no more about the consulting, and frankly I was relieved. If he was as disdainful of my ability to be of service as his insensitive blundering indicated, I didn't want to finalize the argument – yet. I needed time to think about my position relative to what he had just revealed about himself. He was going by the book.

After Sam left, I traded my good clothes for my good-old zip-up robe and sank back into my favorite chair in the Florida room, closed my eyes and breathed in and out deeply ten times. That usually empties me of pointless anger. I get "centered," as the gurus say. Ommmmmm, and so on. But it didn't work this time.

Sam irritated me in a familiar way. The male way. He had not been in my house for more than ten minutes tonight before walking out the back door to talk to his police pals (and one *was* a woman). Of course he was right to wonder why I had not told him anything in my message about finding my own neighbor's corpse. I had deliberately teased him with the invitation to "something special" for dinner. Had I resorted to feminine wiles? He had arrived in his beloved blue T-bird, which he used only for social occasions, and found yellow tapes fluttering around the houses up and down the street, and the green vehicles parked in front of my house. His arrival with a bottle of wine had been witnessed by a dozen neighbors huddled in the street nearby, some with dogs on leashes so as not to appear too obviously nosy. Did I humiliate him?

But I was humiliated, too! And frustrated. One of those

officers out back apparently told Sam right away about the break-in at Urquardt's home. The officers who interviewed me had said it looked like Roland had died from a blow to the back of the head, though it might not have been anything but a fall. Fat chance. Maybe they didn't know about the break-in then. Or maybe they did and just didn't want to alarm me. But why hadn't I even thought to ask more pointed questions? I could have asked if the house had been broken into. It never occurred to me. My mind was still on cartons being delivered. Now I wondered, was the break-in about those cartons?

I would have to work on developing a new persona to get more out of people – become a nosy parker, perhaps. I could wear a big, flower-bedecked hat. No, that's ridiculous. I need their respect. But short of credentials and a paid job, who could I say I am? A journalist? That would be lying. A concerned citizen? Well, yes. And concerned neighbor. I could start right around here. Those officers might not have asked my neighbors the right questions.

I closed my eyes, and willed my mind to come back to the question of what steps a killer might take versus the steps a robber might take. And what about Urquardt himself? Who had he been in his former life that could have motivated either robbery or murder?

The Facts: Urquardt went out for a walk last night or this morning (as yet no one knew quite when), got delivered a blow to his head and wound up in the pond. Period. All the rest was speculation. Scenario Roman Numeral One: A tree branch cracked and fell on him, and no one had thought to look in the water for the debris. Impossible? But I will ask.

Scenario II: The blow was delivered by a petty thief who had waited in the dark (or faint dawn) for someone to stroll by. Scenario II, Motive A: This attacker wanted to rob the walker of whatever was in his pockets and just happened to find the house key which led to further ideas. But if he wasn't waiting for Urquardt specifically, how did he know what house the key unlocked? Scenario II, Motive B: Someone wanted Urquardt-in-particular dead, and the break-in occurred when they entered the house to search for something-in-particular. Maybe the cartons, or whatever was in them. They could have killed Urquardt then and deposited his body in the pond. Hence the broken plant stalks. But why bother taking him to the pond? It's not as if he'd wash out to sea. Scenario II, Motive C: They wanted him dead and waited until he was out walking, then broke into his house to muddy the waters, so to speak. Maybe they didn't intend to kill him, only to detain him. Maybe he stumbled into the pond himself, hitting his head on a rock. But what would he be doing there? If he were night fishing, he would have had tackle. And he wouldn't be wearing a suit and tie.

Scenario III: The murderer went to Urquardt's house to confront him about something and Urquardt ran out the back door and down to the pond to hide. The murderer found him and bashed him in the head out of anger, unpremeditated. The ransacked house was either something the murderer did in his rage, or something that Urquardt did himself in panic. More likely it was the intruder's fallback action, a hunt for something Urquardt wouldn't hand over when he was confronted on his doorstep – or on his walk. Maybe he was supposed to meet someone with something in hand – like an envelope of money, or even cocaine. Maybe that's what was in the cartons.

Why cocaine? Just because it's always in the papers doesn't mean that's the only thing passing from hand to hand illegally. What about diamonds? What about faux Gucci bags? Why not illegally trapped alligators, for that matter?

Scenario IV: It was primarily a robbery. IV, Motive A: the robber turned up not expecting Urquardt to be at home and then had to deal with it. Or IV, B, he was out but the desired item wasn't where it should have been. And where was Urquardt?

Oh, Lord! A lead brick fell into my ruminations. Tonight, I was so caught up in trying to prove to Sam how much help I would be to him that I forgot to tell him about Deborah's "job" offer. Now what could I do? I could already see that "I told you so" smug look on his face. He would drop his eyes and press his mouth into a sort-of smile. The good news was that we might be able to eliminate the possibility that Urquardt was confronted in his house if Deborah was correct, that he hadn't been around all week. If Sam believed her.

The telephone rang. I hated to be distracted now when I was trying to figure out how to present this to Sam, so answered in desultory fashion, ready to make excuses. It was herself: Deborah.

"I'm having an impromptu birthday party tomorrow night."

"What? Even though…?"

"Yes. The neighbors are all in shock. We need some fun. Sophie – are you all right?"

"Yes. I'm fine." I wasn't completely, and I did get her point, but it sounded to me like she had an agenda. "I'm not in shock, anyway."

"Well, you were the one to find the body." She sounded accusatory.

"Yes, but you were his closest neighbor. You seem all right." But how odd, I thought to myself, that someone the neighbors didn't like very much, or in some cases envied, would suddenly offer "first aid" to her critics and detractors. A few hours ago she felt sorry for herself. Besides, with all her talk about needing money, I wasn't sure she could afford to throw a party. Was she playing chameleon once again?

"Well, life goes on," she replied.

I had to agree with that. I asked, "Did you talk to the

police?" I knew it wasn't when they made their rounds, because she had high-tailed it out of the neighborhood.

"They came tonight, asked a few questions, took notes, and left."

"They didn't seem especially interested in your callers?"

"Nope." My suspicion was that she hadn't even told them about the men who asked her to watch Urquardt's house. I was even more convinced when she switched the topic back to my role in his murder.

"It's all over that you were the one who happened to see him floating there in the pond."

"And called the police. If one finds a body in her backyard, that's what one does."

"It must have been so creepy. I'm scared, and I didn't even see him."

"It wasn't a pretty picture."

"Are you alone tonight?"

"Yes, and I'm about to crawl into bed."

"Please, may I come over?"

I wanted to say no, but I also wanted to know what was on her flip-flopping mind. "I guess so, but I am pretty tired."

"I won't stay long. I just need a little friendly company." Three minutes later there was a knock, and I opened the door to a pale shadow of the woman who had kept her looks and hence a series of good-looking boyfriends with sporty-looking cars, and was a confident homeowners' association board member. Her hair was a bird's nest, her face splotchy, and she was wearing a rumpled pink tee-shirt over baggy light blue sweats. And fuzzy yellow slippers. She accepted a gin and tonic (the real reason she may have wanted to visit) and laid her cheek against the cold glass while I sipped my NightyNite tea. She stared out the back window. The moonlight was high in the sky and barely streaming across the pond's rippled surface. The only visible sign of the crime was a long metal stake bearing a flapping orange ribbon that an investigator had pushed into the bank where the body was found.

"I can't believe it – a murder right here in Bridgewater Village." Deborah shivered.

"Deborah, truthfully, how well did you know Roland Urquardt?" She had put the nearly empty glass on the table, and sat now with her freckled suntanned arms crossed over her stomach.

"Not very. Honest. We waved to each other, mostly, like I said. Once in a while I'd see him walking the dog toward Dorado Circle."

"You mentioned the dog this morning. I've never seen him."

"Scout. He kept him in a kennel out back."

"I wonder if he is still there now. Does he bark?"

"I don't know. He was muzzled when I saw him."

"What else do you know about Roland?"

"Well, he hated Spaniards."

"What? Spaniards?"

"Well, you know, the Mexican groundskeepers."

"Oh, you mean Hispanics. How did this subject come up?" It was clear now that they had had more than formal exchanges.

"I saw him chewing them out – the guys who come around the condos, you know."

"Well, that doesn't mean he wouldn't chew out non-Hispanics if they didn't do the job right."

"I was right there. He turned to me and grumbled something about illegal immigrants."

"Did he complain to them regularly?"

"I'm not sure, but I heard them talking when they came to my yard one day, and they made gestures toward his house like they were talking about him. I wonder…It could have been one of them getting even."

"Getting even? Death seems a rather harsh punishment for perhaps justifiable criticism."

"You wouldn't know this, but the people on the Grounds Maintenance Committee who counted the votes said he voted against paying them more per hour. That could have made them mad enough to kill him. If they knew. That's my theory, anyway."

Now I began to wonder if Deborah had a grudge against Urquardt herself. Maybe it was because he refused her attention. Anyway, none of this seemed totally reliable information, as it was obvious to me by now that she had consumed more than the current G&T. But why had she come over at all?

Deborah sat up and hunched forward on the edge of the chaise, her fuzzy-slippered feet flat on the floor, and her hands rubbing together between her knees. She was cold. Was she really still worried about the men in jackets and the mysterious calls, even though Roland was dead? Was she worried that she would have to give their money back? I could believe she wanted to know what the police were thinking and doing, and I would be the person to ask. I wanted to ask her precisely what she had told the police, but was afraid she'd clam up if she hadn't followed my instructions. Instead I hedged and decided to involve her a little in my own thought process.

"Deborah, let's think this through: Had you ever seen anyone else around Roland's house besides the men who unloaded the boxes?"

"He sometimes had visitors at night. Not women, only men. I was beginning to think maybe he was gay."

"Why not just a poker player?"

"Well, it wasn't regular. Besides, he occasionally took off on long weekends. I thought he went fishing out on the ocean. Hank and I spotted him out in the bay." He had been with a group on Tierra Firma II, one of the three fishing boats that could be chartered from the north marina. Her party was on Tierra Firma I. "One of Hank's friends is an expert on it."

"On what?"

"Bringing in the big ones. He's a body-builder, too. And about 80 years old."

I couldn't help but think that her 65th birthday must be weighing on her mind. If you have very little money, but good health, and expected to live 15 or more years, age would be a little worrying.

"Well, you've got the clothes now," I said. You could become a body-builder, too." She laughed.

"I used to be an athlete – in high school track." I let her talk about it, as she seemed to have a need to, and by the time it was half past midnight, her mood seemed to be on the upswing. Also, I now knew Deborah's past: She had grown up in Muncie, Indiana; her dad was a cop and she wanted to be a cop, too, but he wouldn't let her. Then she went to secretarial school, and married too young to her first boss, a shopping mall developer. He died of a heart attack. There was no life insurance.

Then came the shocker. Her future plans.

"I've decided I'm going to go away for a while. I have to rethink my life. After my party, I'm going up north for a while to stay with a cousin. But don't tell anyone. I want to wait until tomorrow night to make the announcement. That way there will be no fuss."

As she waved goodbye, stumbling just a bit on my steps, I thought to myself that our neighbors – and she had invited about 15 – were not likely to miss her. Sad.

Lying in bed at last, I was having a problem reconciling Deborah's Roland, the big time deep sea fisherman, with my Roland, the pond dock caster I had encountered a few times early in the morning. You don't use pond size bait for big tunas, and you don't experiment with tuna bait in ponds. In my mind, the little man seemed much better suited to the small stuff. He was about five feet six, slender, well-coordinated, cheerful enough, but extremely introverted. He looked elderly with his white fringe of hair and gray mustache. And he had pink cheeks. Over a tan. He was sporty-looking. In fact, one reason the necktie had seemed like an odd detail is that he usually wore open-necked shirts and tasseled loafers, even the few times he came to parties. And he never stayed very long. Like the Governor, or President of the United States, he stayed just long enough to be noticed, shook a few hands, did not imbibe or stand around munching canapés like most men did. He seemed never to get into extended conversations.

Roland Urquardt's social life definitely was somewhere else. Around here, it seemed as if he didn't want to stand out in any way. That was one reason I was surprised to hear about his canine companion, and I wondered if it was a recent development, if he felt he needed a guard dog. And, by the way, where was "Scout"?

How important was Deborah in this? Her eagerness to leave Dorado Bay suggested there was more to this than she had already revealed. Or maybe she was really and truly scared those men would return. She had their money. And it certainly was understandable that she'd be genuinely nervous after her closest neighbor had come to such a bad end.

If she was afraid, should I be afraid? It happened in my backyard. I was not happy to realize that something like this could happen in Bridgewater Village. As crime rates in Florida accelerated, there had been many discussions about security, and how hard it was to guarantee the relaxed Florida lifestyle most of us retired people expected, but there was even more concern about property values. Too many new, gated communities were being built these days, so that Bridgewater, once in the vanguard of condo lifestyle, currently had eight unoccupied bungalows. That is to say, no one lived there even part of the year. Many winter residents were gone all during the sticky summer months, but to have "For Sale" signs up for more than a month or two was unheard of until those new gated communities were built. If Deborah was thinking of moving away, this was the worst time to try to sell her home.

Saturday, June 13

"His sister died some time ago," Sam announced. "He didn't tell you?"

"We didn't talk about personal things. He simply mentioned that his sister was a librarian, like me, otherwise, it was just the usual safe topics, comments about weather, nice trim on the grass, had a Blue Heron land in my yard, etcetera."

Sam had knocked on my front door just as I was unplugging the coffee maker, but there were a couple of cups left, so I poured them into mugs and we sat down on the patio, facing the pond. He didn't seem to notice I was not yet dressed. That is, I was still in a faded plaid shirt hanging out over baggy walking shorts. I am self-conscious about my bare arms, they are so age-spotted (not freckled like Deborah's), but his eyes were on the police operations just starting at the pond. Two men in black rubber suits had waded in and now were again probing with poles. What were they looking for? Meanwhile, the uniformed officers of the previous day (one malc and onc female) were still going around to the neighbors.

"Do you have detectives at Mr. Urquardt's house?"

"We have rotations of one. Why do you ask? You sleep all right?"

"Yes. Most of the night, anyway. I got to bed rather late."

It was the perfect opening, so I told him about Deborah's visit last night, and that she was scared because some of Roland's acquaintances had come to her door early yesterday morning to ask if she'd seen him, that he had a fishing date with them and wasn't home when they came to get him, so they were concerned, and they had the impression she was Roland's friend. That's all I said. I really wanted to ask Sam if he had talked to the detectives who had interviewed her. I wished I could find out exactly what she did and didn't tell them, and what they had thought of her, but I didn't dare raise questions that would put her in the spotlight. I needed Deborah to trust me. Of course I needed Sam to trust me, too, but I'd have to let Sam find some things out on his own.

"Come with me, Sam," I said. "Let's go see if she's all right. I was planning on going over anyway to ask if she needed any extra plates and glasses."

"What for?"

"She just turned 65, and she is having a party." Sam raised his eyebrows and shook his head. I added quickly, "She thinks it will take the neighbors' minds off the murder."

"I bet the gossip will blow things all out of proportion. We'll be answering prowler calls over here for months to come."

Deborah was dressed in her sweats but had on makeup this morning. She was cheerfully grateful for my offer, but I could see she was suspicious of Sam's presence. He nodded when I introduced them and she seemed to relax. She asked if we wanted coffee. I accepted, mainly so we could spend more than five minutes with her. She made a half pot and sat down across from Sam at her kitchen table. Much to my surprise, she got to the subject without any prompting.

"Sophie, I suppose you want me to tell Captain Samuels about the two friends of Mr. Urquardt who paid me a visit yesterday morning."

"That might be helpful," Sam replied calmly.

"I've been feeling guilty about that," she continued obliquely, looking downcast. "I should have told the officers who came to ask me questions, but I was afraid of getting involved. And I didn't know their names."

"Do you have any idea how we could find out, Ms. Conyers?" Sam asked.

"They might come back. That's why I'm telling you now. I'm getting scared. Maybe they weren't fishing buddies after all."

"We would have put a watch on your house, Ms. Conyers," Sam said gently.

"I was just hoping it was over when I heard from Sophie that Mr. Urquardt was dead. I think they came to me just because I was the only handy neighbor."

"Are you sure? From what you said these men had the impression you and Roland were buddy-buddy."

"Their coming here had to be a misunderstanding, of mistaken identity. I was not a friend of Roland Urquardt. But I know for sure I can't take a chance. I saw a prowler over there last night after I got home from Sophie's house."

"Where?" Sam asked.

"I'll show you." She led us into her bedroom. "I was closing the curtains at this window and saw a beam of light across the street, in his house. Someone was in there with a flashlight. Roland's floor plan is just like mine, only in reverse. One bedroom faces the front, but across from my kitchen. I could just see a man's back, shoulders, and head."

"It was a police guard," Sam told her. "We have a stakeout."

"With a flashlight?" Deborah paused for a nanosecond and continued. "Anyway, just then the phone rang – it must have been about 1 a.m. – and I picked up the receiver but dropped it when I hit my shin on the bedrail. By the time I got it in my hand again there was nothing but the dial tone."

Sam looked puzzled. I could tell he was beginning to think she was making things up to get attention. Or to mislead him.

"Damn, I've got the jitters!" Deborah went on, forcing a laugh. "And to think I once wanted to be a cop! Good thing Dad stopped me."

I began to understand. She was trying to win him over one way or another. Now it was the dumb blonde talking.

He wouldn't fall for it. I felt for her, though. She had told me the night before about her dad and all the nights her mother lay awake waiting for him to come home, or for someone from the force to come and deliver the bad news. In fact, the tough old cop had outlived his wife. Her mother had died at 39 of cancer, probably brought on by her worrying. Her dad lived eight more years. At a desk. He was 50. Deborah was 27. She had been alone in the world for a pretty long time.

Now she was curled up on a sofa with her hands over her face. Maybe she was faking it a bit, but sighs were coming from somewhere deep inside her. I sat beside her and stroked her hair until she quieted down while Sam looked more impatient than embarrassed.

"The police will continue to be on watch," he finally said. "I'll tell them to watch your house, too."

"I'll check on you later," I promised. "And, by the way, happy birthday. I'm looking forward to the party, and I can help with preparations if you need me."

"I've got a girl coming to help," she answered in a tiny voice.

Well! I thought this was interesting. She could afford that much. But I couldn't let Deborah's erratic behavior distract me from the work ahead. I planned to go back to the library. Sam and I left, reassuring her that the police were on her side, but as we walked out of the cul de sac he was speechless. We noticed a couple more police cars had arrived. We walked through my carport to the patio to see what was going on. I didn't really want him to stick around all morning. I had to get my act together. I was glad, though, that I had thought to take him over to see Deborah. I hoped I had come across as a willing partner, not the dumbbell who forgot to tell him about Deborah's visitors when I first knew of them yesterday.

"Are you nervous – about staying here alone at night?" Sam asked me.

"Oh no. Although I admit I stayed awake a long time thinking about Roland's tie. It was so unusual, so unnatural, and so…wiggly." Sam just grunted. I hate that kind of response.

"Apparently, whatever happened, it happened late at night and not early in the morning," he said. "That tie should have told us right away that he was coming home from an engagement, not going fishing." No doubt his team had gone through all my scenarios in about ten minutes. I then remembered the dog.

"Deborah said she sometimes saw Roland walking a dog," I mentioned. Sam didn't know if anyone had found a dog at the house. I could tell he was not giving Deborah's stories much credibility.

"The dog that didn't bark," I murmured.

"What?"

"You know – Sherlock Holmes." I explained the reference.

"Oh, yeah. I remember something about that," he said. "I'll ask about the dog when I get back."

"Maybe he's loose in the neighborhood," I suggested. "His name is Scout. He probably has tags. Roland struck me as that kind of person."

Sam was quiet the next few minutes, still staring at the men in the pond. "I've been thinking about what you offered," he finally said.

"What was that?"

"Consulting. I can agree to one thing." I held my breath. "I can agree to giving you the assignment to ask around the neighborhood, you know, find out about this victim and – well, be nosy. In your own way. I'll pay you out of my discretionary funds. A couple hundred to start."

I had to bite my tongue, wanting to say I preferred the arrangement to be in the open and to be professional, but I didn't want to blow my chances altogether. To be honest, I felt a little thrill run up my arms. I was free now to tell him more about Deborah.

"There are some things Deborah told me that she didn't mention this morning. Little details she left out. I asked if her visitors were Anglos and she said she thought they were Italians. Why Italians? She said they wore leather jackets." I laughed to let him think I didn't take it seriously.

"Profiling," Sam grunted.

"I should have told her leather jackets have no cultural boundaries. My own son has one."

Now Sam was laughing. That was good. So I told him about the other men she had seen going into his house at night.

"She said they all wore those jackets, and that there were at least six or eight different men stopping by at night in groups of two or three over a few months." He stopped laughing.

"My God. She is a natural to ask to watch a neighbor's house. It sounds like she had her nose pressed to the window all the time."

"Not that bad. I think she sits out on her carport on a folding chair at night. That's how she noticed they came in a few different models of car but they were always black cars." Sam guffawed this time as if he couldn't quite believe that story.

"Deborah said, Deborah said. Do you think this woman is believable?" Now I thought he sounded disappointed in me, not her. I relied too much on secondhand information.

"She may dramatize a bit."

"Why do you believe her? Because she's female?"

"No. Because she's the daughter of a cop."

"No you are profiling. I've never told you about my kids." I didn't expect him to tell me now. I just wanted him to go so I could think. Maybe Deborah was dramatic, but I thought I could justify my belief in her.

"Maybe so," I replied evenly, "but she has good ears, and good eyes." I hoped he'd take that as a token of my esteem for police training. "Remember, she was planning to follow in his footsteps," I added. Sam just rolled his eyes.

At two o'clock I saw the florist's van turn into the cul de sac, and when it left I walked over with a box of tall plastic glasses and found Deborah in a lighter mood. Bags of goodies were all lined up on the bar and she was putting groceries in the fridge. She had already set out bowls and platters for the party. Three long, narrow, green boxes were laid on her kitchen table, one open. It was full of long stemmed roses.

"My, how gorgeous!" I said, and then, less tactfully, "Who on earth sent all these to you"

"I did. Well, why not? No one else was going to do it for me."

"Great idea!"

"How about a G&T to get started?"

"Too early for me," I replied. "I'll toast you with water, though. She poured me the water with a slice of lemon and herself a tall glass, half gin, with lime.

"To 65-year-old you," I said. "Still young and gorgeous."

She drank deeply, sitting on the bar stool. The fan lifted the corners of the cute paper napkins stacked on the bar. Each one contained a joke about memory. I remarked on those.

"Well, my memory is still pretty good. Memories I have. Memory rich." She looked down into her glass and her mood changed. "Hank left me nothing but memories, you know. No Uzzi Magnani beach house, no $500,000 CD, and not even the dark green XJ6 Series III classic convertible he drove. We made many arrivals together in that, impressing the young valets. Well now I know. And his brother paid the balance on his funeral and burial."

"I'm so, so sorry," I said automatically.

"You said that," she snapped. Yes, she did have a good memory.

"Of course it would be a burial. No scattering of ashes for Henry Harding Lane Norris, which, as it turned out, was not even his birth name. It was Larry Harding. I found his address book in a drawer in a desk after I called 911. His brother was listed there as an emergency contact, on page one: John Harding. I called him. He didn't get here in time for the service, which I arranged, of course, but he came a few days later and told me the brutal facts."

This time I said nothing.

"You're not the only one who finds bodies, Sophie George," she said to me, bitterness in her voice. She dumped her lime and ice into the sink and poured herself straight gin.

"I'm sorry, too," she then said. "But I'll get over it." Then she turned toward me and said, "No I won't. Even if I live to have Alzheimer's. Hank – or Larry – with a plastic bag over his head. It's too big a thing. I'll have nightmares in the nursing home. Gawd! They'll have to straitjacket me."

"Do you want to tell me about how it happened?" I asked. "It might help." She nodded, I thought eagerly.

On that Friday, the usual day of their assignation, Deborah had driven to the *Neo-Modern* house with its rounded corners and layers of white-piped decks that clung to the side of a cliff. I knew the house. Everyone who knew the swankier parts of Dorado Bay did. It had been very elaborately engineered. Deborah explained its layout: You couldn't see much of it from the street or even the driveway. At street level, there was the garage, and beside the garage there was a gate and steps leading to a wooden footbridge that crossed a gully to the house and the main floor decks. That's how most visitors would arrive. Deborah had an automatic opener for the garage, and would park inside. She took a route that led to a windowless door hidden behind a profusion of bougainvillea. It let her into an exercise room and a few feet down a hallway there was another door that opened into a dressing room. That was adjoined to the master bedroom. Deborah said Hank called this sequence of doorways his escape route. More precisely, it was her escape route, for she had used it many times to get out of that private part of the house when he had unexpected other guests. She added with venom: "As far as the rest of the world knew, we were just 'good friends'."

Hank had arranged to meet her there at five p.m., but Deborah was early. She contemplated having a long soak in the spa tub and then decided a quick swim in the pool would be nicer. She kept her bathing suit in a drawer in the dressing room bureau. Slipping it on, she stepped through to the bedroom, usually darkened by closed shutters, and found the room bathed in bright afternoon light. The shutters were folded back, and the sliding door to the balcony was open, too. She peeked out and started to call his name when she had a feeling that someone else was in the room. She turned and saw Hank lying on the enormous four-columned bed, wearing his clothes and the white plastic bag molded to his head. A bottle containing about an inch of bourbon was on the bedside table, and several pill bottles lay uncapped and empty on the floor where, it appeared, he had dropped them. Deborah said it felt to her like time had stopped. It was absolutely still in the room. She yelled for help, but there was nobody in the house or living close by. All she could hear in response was the crying of gulls and fluttering of roosting birds.

So that was that, Hank's ultimate grand statement. The

police came and went. She found the address book and called the brother. Made plans for a memorial service. Then when the brother showed up to clear up the estate, the facts tumbled out, one disappointment after another. But, in the end, what hurt the most was her realization that their friendship had not been enough to keep him going and maybe one day recognize that he might as well 'fess up and stop telling her those outrageous lies. They could put their bits and pieces together, live in one house, and take care of each other.

I expressed my sympathy by putting my arms around her as she hid her face behind her hands. And now what? She was still young by today's standards, but too old to find a job.

"How bad is your financial outlook?" I asked boldly. She told me her dribble of income from her father's insurance was subsidized by her own meager social security payments – enough to buy food and pay the rent. But there were the utility bills, the car expenses, and medical costs. She was in pretty good shape now, but the blood pressure pills, hormones, calcium, B6, and the occasional mood adjusters cost about $200 a month. Her car was old, like mine, and likely to need repairs. How long could she keep that up?

"Any extravagances?" I prodded.

"I'm not looking forward to giving up my gin. I need it more than ever." She laughed. "And I need to buy a few nice clothes, unless all my dates are with mall walkers." She laughed again and I tried to laugh with her.

I now understood. When Hank died, she felt betrayed. Everything seemed to be over for her here in Dorado Bay. She was really in a slump. Then came the men with their job offer, paying a thousand dollars a month. She saw relief for a while, and then a few hours later she got the phone calls and started worrying. And then I arrived with the news of Roland's murder. The big, scary question was how much the visits and calls from those men had to do with his demise.

"Deborah, what did you tell the police, exactly?"

She conceded that when the police finally found her at home in the evening she hadn't said anything at all about the men and their offer. When they asked if she had noticed anything unusual going on across the street, she just shook her head.

She told me she had not slept well that night. She lay eyes wide open looking at the fan turning slowly, just like I do some nights, the negative thoughts turning and turning.

"I understand how disappointed you must be," I told her. "I wonder, though, if being alone so much of the time since Hank died hasn't made you overly sensitive.

"That's what I was thinking when the investigators came to talk to me. As you said, someone delivering packages to a neighbor is not unusual. Also, I don't remember the exact date. Was it two weeks ago? A month? If I remembered – maybe had kept my receipts for my groceries that afternoon,

I would have told them anyway. And if they had asked me straight out if anyone had come to my house looking for Roland, I might have told them. But, honestly, Sophie, telling the police about their offer seemed too risky. I'd sound crazy. Nothing made sense. Do we know for sure that these things were connected? Besides, there was the money I'd already accepted. The police might want the money as evidence. I had already spent some of it on my party."-

"Oh, Deborah...." That's all I could say. It was the money again. I did think the way those men had behaved was suspicious. Could they be the killers? It didn't seem that way. They had talked as if Roland was going to be around for a while, for her to watch. And they said they would be back. They didn't say when. Come to think of it, whatever they expected her to see would not have to involve Roland Urquardt at all. It could still happen, whatever it was. Or maybe his death put an end to whatever they were doing. Or maybe she was making it up.

"Why did they have to involve me?" Deborah wondered aloud as I sat thinking about these contradictions. "What made them think I had a friendship with their buddy, possibly gay, or possibly, considering those boxes, a drug dealer?"

I was most confounded by the calls. According to Deborah, they made no direct reference to the men's visit and they occurred on the very day of the murder but did not talk about Roland specifically. Was his murder "the sign"?

Sign of what? What was she expected to do? Would they call again?

"The only reason I told you those things, Sophie, is that you're a smart woman. I thought you might scold me. But I didn't think you'd betray me."

"I don't think I did," I replied, yet not sure.

"I told you they wanted my answer by noon. Why didn't you tell me to just say no? Spend all day watching out the window? What kind of life is that?"

"Which reminds me to ask you, did you call your prospective employers when you saw the prowler?"

"I don't have their phone numbers," she said, looking intently at her freshly painted fingernails. The way she saw it now, she needed to get away from here. It would be dangerous to sit in her window. She wasn't going to hide, but a change of scenery would be good. She could go anytime she wanted after the party was over.

"There's no rush to come back, either," she concluded.

Millie's was open for just another hour and a half. My excuse for popping in was to find something to wear for the party. Millie suggested a satin dress with overly wide shoulders. It was more costume than clothing. There were three or four more of this ilk that she insisted I try on, even though I knew I wouldn't buy them. It was damned hard work, all kinds of infrastructure to figure out, lots of little buttons on the sleeves, all the time with Millie tugging and smoothing. Time was going by too quickly.

"The party is a little more casual an affair than these lovely dresses suggest," I said, not adding that I thought they were priced out of my range.

"This one is very smart," Millie said, holding up a canary yellow jacket and skirt, and twice the price I wanted to pay. "I had Bettina Vander-Smythe in mind when I ordered it," she said. I didn't know whether I should be flattered or not. Was Millie putting me in the same class with the popular pharmaceuticals heiress, or saying the suit was a reject, the heiress didn't like it?

"Find me something not so pushy," I suggested. Millie nodded and brought in a lavender outfit that was feminine and fitted. It, too, was a dash sophisticated for Bridgewater events, but I tried it on and stood before the mirror, twisted sideways and looked at the way the jacket curved in at my waist and laid smoothly over my nether parts. The skirt fell to well below my knees and was pencil slim except for a bottom tier that was very slightly ruffled. My heart skipped a beat. It was expensive, but it would never go out of style. I could wear it to my funeral.

"Not what you'd expect to see on a retired librarian," I joked, more than a little embarrassed to be shopping for a murder assignment. "The color is lovely." Looked at closely, it actually was soft gray with a fine rose and blue abstract pattern.

"Luscious Italian fabric." Millie looked at her watch. "You have time to stop in at Firenza for some gray pumps," she added, without actually seeming to look at my favorite tan walking shoes that Monty used to call my "boats."

"I don't have time today," I replied. "I have to stop at the library."

"I thought you'd retired."

"I did quit my library job, but I am still assisting a private client who wants to know something about the Urquardt family for a project he's working on."

"Oh, yes, the art patron. If that's the one you mean. You know there were a few wonderfully scandalous members of that family, and I don't know where they've gone."

"Is the art patron still alive? He would be pretty old – in his 90s, if the paper's facts were right."

"I don't know. I haven't heard anything about him in years and years. Rudolph, I think, was the art patron's name. He had two sons by two different marriages. The elder joined his father's business but died young of a heart attack. The other worked in Washington for a law firm. Like their father, neither could keep their wives. I think the old man deliberately scared them off!"

"Thank you," I said. "That's helpful."

"I wouldn't be telling you this if there were any Urquardts

still living in Dorado Bay," Millie said, keeping her reputation intact. She apparently had not read the afternoon paper. She'd find out tonight on TV, if she watched the news.

While Millie carefully folded my new dress around a cushion of tissue paper, and gently laid it in one of her signature gold boxes, she gossiped more generally about the "Euro trash" moving in, anorexic second and third wives of the new multi-millionaires from Russia and Saudi, who razed the early 20th century Mediterranean villas to build post-modern fortresses on the beach.

"They want clothes fresh off the runways," Millie grumbled.

"They need to show that their husbands have made it," I suggested.

"They're barely in their thirties," Millie threw in. "They've got a lot to learn."

"I never see them in the library," I quipped, suspecting Millie, twice-divorced, was thinking these pseudo-socialites' carefree lives would not last.

"They are too busy jetting back and forth from Paris to London to New York," she said. Ahhh, the competition was on her mind.

"You'd think they'd want a good read for their trip."

"They pick up *People* and read about themselves," was Millie's final shot. It seemed to me Millie was getting a little bitter in her old age. Well, don't we all?

The library was closed. I had taken too long jabbering. It occurred to me that I might have been Millie's only customer that day, and I didn't even know her last name. She might be lonely, too. Nonetheless, as I drove home I wondered how I could be so cold-blooded as to go shopping for myself right after viewing the body of an acquaintance, apparently murdered. Perhaps it was the shock. No, it was calculated. This was a turning point in my relationship with the chief detective, the point that would determine how I spent the next few years of my life. When I hung my new outfit on the door of the closet, I noticed that Millie had also stuffed tissue paper into the sleeves, something younger shop girls wouldn't know how to do. Good for her, I thought. I would call and thank her.

The phone rang, and it was Sam, asking me to meet him for a quick bite to eat. He wanted to talk. I just about had time to get dressed for the party and spend an hour or so with him. Since we still weren't comfortable with my role, I didn't want to put him off. Besides, I needed to know if he had found out anything about Deborah's potential employers.

Sam was sitting at the corner table drumming his fingertips on its Formica top. I walked over to him with a confident stride. My new dress felt wonderfully swishy. But he was frowning as if he didn't approve. Of course, I was more than a few minutes late.

"Sam, I'm sorry..."

"For what?"

"I'm so late."

He glanced at his watch and raised his eyebrow. "Time flies when you're having fun," he muttered. "What do you want to drink?"

"Just iced tea. I have miles to go before I sleep." I smiled and rested my wrists against the table, and glanced down at the menu. He beckoned the rail-thin, teenage waiter and asked for the tea.

"I've been sitting here thinking," he said. "What have I gotten myself into this time? Having you poke around the Internet is one thing, but to poke around Dorado Bay – well – there are a few shady goings on that perhaps the mysterious Roland Urquardt was in on, at least the fringe. Hell, maybe he was in the middle. If that was the case, lady wannabe detective, I'm guilty of putting you in danger."

I didn't answer until he pounded his fist on the tabletop. In order not to draw attention to our booth I just said, "We don't know enough yet to think such things."

"And why are you wasting all your time on that airhead neighbor?"

"Maybe it is a waste of time," I admitted. "But right now she needs reassurance. I'm her only friendly neighbor." I had decided not to let him know that Deborah was planning on going away. He would be all too pleased.

"You seem to be going someplace fancy," he said.

"Deborah's birthday party."

"It's a dressy affair?"

"Champagne and Princess cake."

"I thought I would be your escort," he said, "but I look like a slob. You should have warned me." I read between the lines that he was annoyed not to be invited. I had never even considered it.

"It's just neighbors. I'm hoping to find out if any of them know any more about Roland Urquardt than we've found out so far."

"And what is your plan of action?"

"Depends on what I hear – little details add up."

"You're determined to make this complicated, are you?"

"You're determined to make it simple, are you?" I responded.

"I am ninety-nine and nine-tenths percent sure it was a robbery."

"Based on what evidence?"

"The break-in. What else do you need?"

"I look at things in their broader context."

"Don't push it, Ms. George. If you begin to mess around in other matters and the chief super hears about it, I'll have to pull your badge,"

"My badge?"

"Well, you know; my permission."

This hit me hard. He still hadn't bought into our

agreement. He still didn't trust me, value my insights. I decided to say nothing. He seemed to be asking for a fight and I wasn't giving it to him. The waiter came back and took our orders. Sam again drummed his fingers on the table. It was time for détente. I smiled sweetly and reached out to cover his fingers with my hand.

"Sam. I don't want you to be nervous on my behalf; I'm a big girl now."

"You aren't very big, but even if you were, your ideas are bigger. That's what makes me nervous." If he only knew how nervous *I* was, breaking new ground, trying to adjust the balance of power in our relationship. What could I say that wouldn't upset him? I was going to the party without him because no way was I going to settle for vandalism as the verdict. I was absolutely convinced something very different was behind Urquardt's death. Something very dark. Why else would he have been dumped in the pond? That was a statement. The gauntlet thrown down. I decided to probe Sam's thinking on that.

"Why would he have been dumped in the pond?" I asked, as if just mildly curious.

"Hell, I don't know. Because it was there?" He seemed to snicker. That's when I couldn't help myself. I was ready to suggest the most dramatic scenario, whether he laughed at it or not.

"There is something here like old-fashioned gang warfare,

in my opinion."

"What gives you that idea? We keep tabs on gangs in my department, if you hadn't realized that."

"If I find out more I will tell you," I promised. Settled. The orders arrived. I defied etiquette and tucked my napkin into the "V" of my expensive neckline, spreading it as far as I could across my jacket, even though the chicken salad looked dry. I had trouble keeping it on my fork. Captain Rueben Samuels chomped on a dripping Reuben sandwich.

"My husband Monty and I used to hunt for the ideal Reuben, Rueben" I mentioned with humor I thought might break the ice. He took another bite and nodded to let me know he was listening. "The best was in New Orleans, of all places."

"Why not? New Orleans is known for its good food."

"But not deli food," I said, "not New York food," then let the subject drop. There were enough issues in the air. Sam then flicked some sauerkraut off his cuff.

"There's a bit on your tie," I whispered. There wasn't, of course, but it gave me another opening. "Reminds me – that tie of Urquardt's is a mystery, don't you think?"

"What way?" Munched down again on rye.

"The motif?" I posed it as a question he had to answer. Sam furrowed his brow, wiped his chin with his napkin.

"What motive?"

"*Motif.* Design. I looked at it through binoculars. It was

men on horses. They looked medieval. And evil, too."

"Poet and you don't know it." He resumed chewing, his eyes steady on my face.

"Well, I just thought it was a peculiar choice."

"A lot of my own ties are peculiar. Old girlfriends gave 'em to me." It was my turn to make faces. I arched an eyebrow unbelievingly to mock him. In fact, I was taken aback to think of Sam as having *girl*friends.

"Just kidding. I have a lotta old ties, too wide or too narrow, too fancy, too greasy. You know."

"Well, his was so… well, it looked deliberately eye-catching. And I'd never seen him wearing a tie before."

"Sometimes we have to, as for instance to attend weddings and funerals."

"But I can't imagine why anyone would want to wear a tie looking so menacing to either one of those events – or even to a meeting."

"Urquardt apparently did," said Sam. "It may have been a private joke."

"Exactly my thought – .a message tie."

"An old school tic," he added. Yuk, yuk.

This made me think. I couldn't leave that idea alone. Finally I said, "Did you happen to see the label?" Sam wiped his chin. "Nope." He made a motion to let me know he was going to the men's room.

I had had enough of the salad and sat with my hands

folded on my lap so the teenage waiter would come and take it away. I looked across the room at the view out the plate glass window. In the last few minutes the clouds had become dark, and the streetlight hanging on a wire across the four-lane road swayed. I leaned back against the leatherette chair-back and thought about the hardboiled detective novels given settings like this. In each corner was a banquette. *Banquette.* You hardly every hear anyone use that word these days. It's a "booth." When and why had the French term left the American lingo? And what was the origin of "booth"? Booth. Booth. The more I said it the funnier it sounded. Aha. Named after a Mr. Booth, no doubt the inventor. I hoped it wasn't the same Booth who shot Abraham Lincoln.

Caught up in my silly mind game so typical of librarians, I leaned back to rotate my shoulders and felt a brush on the top of my head. It was, I knew without looking, the feathery plant that separated the room of tables from the corridor leading to the restrooms down a hallway. Then I heard what sounded like Sam's basso tones. It seemed he was repeating to someone what I had just said to him. He was using the pay phone in the restroom hallway.

"The woman who found…had noticed…tie, medieval something. Got me thinking. Look up in . . . apocalypse . . . crazy, but I know I saw it somewhere before . . . check the label? . . . be in later." Obviously, it was a call that couldn't wait until he got back into his phone-equipped car. When he returned, I tried not to smile triumphantly. He sat down with a thump and braced himself with two hands, pushing his face over the table looking fatherly in a bulldoggish way.

"You were on the phone," I said, probingly. "What's happening?"

"I'm pulling you off this case, Sophie. I made a mistake to let you get involved. This thing is going in another direction. Nasty business. Did I tell you they found out this guy had a scar across his belly?

"Mr. Urquardt?"

"Yes. It wasn't an appendectomy."

My mouth went dry and my face started to heat up; I hoped it didn't look red. Sam knew all along we were looking at more than a simple case. I faked a chuckle and, smart aleck that I am, replied, "But what about gall bladder?"

"Nope. Someone tried to disembowel him."

"Maybe during a war? There will be a record of that. In any case, I think you need me even more now, to speed things up."

"Sophie, it – this case – is nothing for a nice librarian. Dr. Batson told me it looks like some sawbones sewed it up. In other words, it was a gang job. He was a mess."

"But he was so small," I said without thinking. The idea of that neat little man being disfigured by surgical torture made me sad. My eyes filled with tears for Roland and maybe for Deborah, if she was still in danger. Fortunately, Sam did not notice my distress. He was digging around in his jacket pockets for his billfold.

"Anyway, you are wayyyyy too distracting. Especially in that, uh, sort-of slinky outfit." He leered at me! But was it a real leer, or pretend?

"Distracting? What does that mean?" I couldn't believe what he was saying. Such stupid remarks were just meant to offend, to keep me out of his way. What a betrayal! Hadn't he just confirmed by his conversation with someone on the phone that my ideas were useful? Or was I going deaf? Hadn't he repeated my very concerns? Was he going to take the credit for my brainwork?

"It means that our relationship, now that you've retired from the library, should be more, well, social." This time he smiled paternalistically. I almost preferred the leer.

"But I haven't retired from thinking!" My eyes now, I am ashamed to say, were brimming for myself, about to send trails down my cheeks. Damn! I kept my ankles tight together to prevent myself from kicking him in the shins under the table. I wanted to have a full tantrum – but knew I could not show that I could get so emotional about it. About what? The grisly killing? Sam's insults? At the same time, a small voice inside me said he at least thought my dress made me look sexy, well, slinky. And I despised myself for the thought.

"No? Well, then, you deserve a rest," he concluded. "Meanwhile, why don't you take me with you to that party?"

"Not a chance," I snapped, swiping my tears away with my napkin. I slid out from under the table and opened my purse, threw a twenty on the table, and stalked away. Before leaving the restaurant, I thought I'd use the restroom and repair my makeup, pull myself together. There was someone else on the phone with his back toward me as I passed by, but I heard him clearly.

"She's got a bee up her ass about the necktie," the excited though hushed voice said. Pause. "Whatever. I'm not a English teacher. Anyway, she told him. He phoned in a request for research." I stepped around the corner where, fortunately, there was a niche for newspaper machines. Pause. "Yeah. Well, what should we do now that I didn't?" Pause. "What about the blonde dame?" Pause. "It'll be easy to get her outta here. But what if somebody finds out before we do who it was killed Urquardt?"

I had planned to go home first and change out of the "slinky" dress. It might put my neighbors on guard and maybe keep them from saying things they would say to the frumpy Sophie George. But I'm not frumpy, I argued. I am conservative, but not altogether without fashion sense.

Hadn't I remembered my old patent sling-back pumps, stored for years on a high closet shelf, would look great with this dress? I pulled into my carport, locked my car, and walked, shoulders back, toward Deborah's house, which by now was rocking off its foundation with laughter and loud greetings of the guests who had the most drinks under their belts. All the immediate neighbors would be there, so there would be no one to complain about the noise.

I was met at the front door by one of the other former Bridgewater association board members, an insurance salesman I had avoided time and time again at gatherings like this. He liked to liven up a conversation with horror stories about claims against homeowners – somebody slipped and fell on the wet sidewalk, was poked in the eye by a tree branch, drowned in a spa. He was accustomed to my cool reception and let me slide by the group that blocked passage through the hallway to the kitchen. Slipping quickly around the corner, into the Florida room and back into the living room, I smiled at everyone, seeking the clique of single females most likely to be talking about the murder. They had taken the most comfortable seats in the house and I joined them, perching on an ottoman. It was pleasant in here, fresh and scented by a huge bouquet of long-stemmed roses sitting on the low cocktail table between two matching sofas. Deborah's gift to herself.

"Sixty of them – or more," Marsha Rheingold said,

expecting that I was making mental calculations like everyone else. She won't tell us exactly how many there are – or who they came from." A professionally printed banner, blue and silver, had been hung on the wall between windows: HAPPY BIRTHDAY, DUCHESS. A couple of unicorns made of cardboard had been scotch-taped to either end.

"Isn't the unicorn suggestive of…I wonder who…" a male coming into the room suggested.

"Hush!" murmured his wife. "You know her boyfriend just died."

"Committed suicide," someone else murmured.

"You don't say! I didn't even know she had someone special," the male newcomer protested. "Hey! Carter! Did you hear that?" He turned back to the all-male crowd in the foyer. Men could be gossips, too.

I got up and walked over to the wide front window facing Roland Urquardt's house. There were no lights, but the yellow tape was still in place.

"Awful to think about, isn't it?" I said to Maeve Murphy, sitting in the nearest chair.

"He was a sour old man," Maeve replied.

"Really? I thought he was pleasant enough when we chatted out by the pond."

"I tried to get him to contribute to the fund for the new craft house. Awful, the way he looked me up and down as if I had no business even asking."

"What did he say?"

"He said, 'Sorry, not this time.'" Maeve pantomimed a door shutting in her face.

"That doesn't seem sour, exactly. He maybe had other charities in mind."

"I just didn't like him. He was abrupt. Anyway, my dad told me he was a crook."

"Your dad?"

"He died just two years ago. That's why I'm here, came down with him to nurse him. Not that he needed me, what with his girlfriends hanging all around the sickbed."

"Really?" I was almost distracted by this salacious story. She probably wanted to tell me more about her dad. But I asked, "What kind of crook was Urquardt – did he say?"

"He was with a law firm that was doing stuff overseas, kind of dodgy. They were very secretive, but a couple of them got knocked off. Dad knew about it because he was a lawyer, too. He heard things in his circle, but he wasn't one to gossip."

"Excuse me, I'm going to the…you know," I said, ducking into the hallway. I stayed in the powder room long enough to let the dynamics change in the front room and then shot out through the kitchen to the backyard. Two golfers who knew me through my late husband sat on a low wall surrounding a fountain. Arch Innes saw me coming and patted a place beside him.

"Long time no see, Sophie," he said. He ogled me in a friendly way. "You look great! I hope Monty is looking down from Heaven."

"Yes, it has been awhile, Arch. Keeping busy?" Arch must be around 90, but still owned a hardware store on the bay near the bridge. His children ran it. His heart hadn't been in the business after his wife died – besides, she had been the bookkeeper – and things were looking pretty muddled after a few months. The kids didn't want to give this cash cow up, so they all moved to Florida from some town in the Midwest.

"More than ever, but I have the two boys helping out."

"That's good." We recalled funny incidents from the days when Beatrice was alive, working the cash register. They were already in their sixties then. Arch sighed.

"Too bad about Roland Urquardt," he said with sincerity in his voice.

"It must be quite a shock to his friends," I agreed. "Did you know him?"

"He came in the store for his fishing gear."

"So he was a serious fisherman?"

"Yeah. At least he bought expensive tackle. Said some of it was for his dad."

"His dad?"

"The old man apparently pretended to fish, long after he was able to step into the boat. He'd cast off the dock at his big home out there on the Gulf."

"Where on the Gulf, Arch? Did you ever see it?"

"Oh I think it was around the bend, near Old Harbor."

"Near downtown?"

"Yeah. But on an island. He invited me there but I never did go. He pointed it out on the aerial photo in the store."

"If I come in, will you show me?" I asked. He nodded, but looked at me in an odd way, as if I were ghoulish in this request.

I kept working the crowded rooms the rest of the evening, darting in where someone had detached himself or herself long enough to engage in private conversation. At a little after midnight, Deborah was at the door saying good-night to each and every guest, murmuring appreciation for their attendance and gifts. When it was my turn to pass through the doorway she pulled me aside.

"I hear you've been asking questions about Roland."

"Who told you that?"

"Everybody. Maeve, Arch, Earlie." Earlie was the neighbor on the other side of Roland. He was deaf as a post and had claimed not to even know who Roland was. "I hope you left me out of it. I don't want anyone to know I might have talked to him." I wanted to shake my finger in her face and say, *Naughty, naughty. You know you should have told the police.* But I decided to let it go and just nodded. I wasn't sure how far to trust her now. She had seemed shaken to the core by the suicide of her boyfriend, Hank, and here she was behaving like a party girl.

She must have known some of the women guests had been repeating rumors about Hank taking on a false identity to prey on people. They said since Deborah certainly wasn't a rich widow when they met that it must have been her looks that got him interested in her – unless they were in it together. I peered into the hostess's tired eyes, smiling but smudged with eyeliner.

"I promised Sam I would ask around," I said.

"The Captain's got you helping on this case?"

I didn't like her look of surprise, as if I were unworthy of being taken into police confidence. I replied tartly, "Of course. I'm a veteran researcher, am I not?" A flush came into Deborah's cheeks, and she leaned forward grabbing my arm tightly.

"Be careful, Sophie. There were things about Roland that scared me. Please don't get too involved." I couldn't have been more dumbfounded. What was this about?

"Do you have something more to tell me?"

"Um, no. I'm not that sure of anything. It's just that I can't understand why he was so secretive." She shook her head without saying more.

"Do you really mean secretive, Deborah, or was he just not very friendly? Look at the facts."

"I know what you are saying. I felt slighted, I admit. But

I still wonder, and I worry about you. Remember, I'm a cop's daughter. Bad stuff happens to nice people. To smart people, too."

"Don't worry. I know my limits, Deborah. I've got Sam to do the rough stuff. But thanks."

As I crossed over the cul de sac I heard Deborah say to some women behind me that she would be leaving Dorado Bay for a vacation tomorrow afternoon and would return when she felt rested. Those who now knew about her boyfriend's tragic death wished her safe journey and good times then quietly disassembled.

I walked around Dorado Circle in the dark thinking about Deborah's comments. As I got to my driveway Sam pulled up beside me with the window rolled down and, imitating a B-movie lothario, softly called, "Wanna take a ride, Gorgeous?" I waved him off, but he cut his motor and got out. I kept on walking toward my front door. He was at my elbow and said, "I'm sorry I let my macho get the best of me." He then explained that he was upset when I left the restaurant, annoyed that I didn't want him to go with me to the party, but was determined not to chase after me. Now I've changed my mind." By then I was trying to unlock my door. I didn't want him in my house, so I just stood there without opening it.

"I was feeling lousy," he went on. "My ears were doing that cricket thing. Damned irritating. Anyway, I stayed there in the restaurant long enough to regain my sense. I kept playing back the exchange we had and felt bad about it. I was only trying to protect you. I like you too much to send you into danger. And it is going to get dangerous. Urquardt seems to have been away from home quite a bit, the kind who would be easily robbed. But if he was the grandson of a man known to have mafia connections, well, that changes the way we have to look at this situation."I was about to ask him to expound on the mafia connection when we both saw a shadowy figure across the street in the cul de sac. Deborah, still in her lipstick red party pantsuit, walked quickly from her driveway to the Urquardt front yard, ducked under the yellow caution tape, and continued along the side of the garage toward the back.

"What's she doing there?" Sam whispered.

"How do I know?" I whispered back. "Taking out the trash?" It was common for neighbors to use the recycling bins of neighbors when the bottles were overflowing in their own. But she didn't have anything in her hands and she moved steadily past the Urquardt bins. We stood on the dark porch and waited. Nothing happened immediately. No lights went on anywhere on the Urquardt property. There was no shouting of a guard. And Deborah did not come back.

"Maybe she is just taking a walk," I suggested, mulling over the possibility that she had a key to Urquardt's back patio doors for some reason she hadn't told me. But why no lights? Where was the police watch?

A more terrible thought came into my mind. Deborah must know something about the unfriendly little fisherman she hadn't told me. She might even be covering any evidence of her own involvement with his activities.

"She's coming back." Sam only mouthed the words this time, poking me in the ribs with his elbow. We watched Deborah emerge from the shadows carrying a cardboard carton about half the size of a countertop microwave. The flaps stood open.

"What do you suppose she has in there?" Sam asked. "Kittens?" That made me smile, but I doubted Roland would have had a cat. But it did look as if something were alive in the box. Or fragile. Deborah was being very careful with it.

"I doubt it's kittens," I said. "Roland had a big dog, remember. Scout. Still no sign of him?"

"Whoever killed Urquardt must have taken the dog away," Sam replied.

"What could she have in there?" I suddenly felt very stupid. Maybe booze, I conjectured, meanly. Perhaps Deborah knew where Roland kept his gin, maybe in a storage shed back there.

"I could arrest her, you know," Sam said, looking for my reaction.

"Don't. Just watch." But Sam started to advance on

Deborah as if intending to intercept her before she got into her house. She apparently heard him, looked back over her shoulder, and hastened her pace.

"How do!" Sam said cheerfully, nodding. "Do you need a hand?"

"No thanks, it's not heavy," Deborah said, ducking into her garage.

"Stay out of the crime scene, don't forget."

She turned briefly, and he nearly caught up with her just as she was pushing the button to keep him on the outside.

Sam turned abruptly and soon was back at my side. He blew out a deep breath.

"What was it?"

"It looked like a bird. I could see what looked like wing sticking up over the top of the box."

"But where did it come from? How did she get in the house?"

"It might have been in a cage on his patio or somewhere else outside. Maybe she knew about it and decided to rescue it."

"Why wouldn't she take the cage?"

"I suppose it was too big. Or maybe it didn't live in a cage."

"Why wouldn't the detectives who searched her property have seen it?"

"Yeah. I wonder, too. I'll ask them in the morning."

"And don't forget about the dog."

Sunday, June 14

I was walking my two miles as usual at 6 a.m. when I saw lights on in Deborah's house and wondered if she had forgotten to turn them off after the party. Or maybe she was too scared to sleep with all the lights off. She was probably still fast asleep. But, no – I could see a shadow passing back and forth behind the curtains, or possibly two shadows. Then I saw the car parked across the cul de sac from her house. It was a black Mercedes, the largest model, not anything likely to be owned by Bridgewater residents. Something else was different on the street. A sandwich board sign now stood sentry in front of the Urquardt property with the message: "DO NOT ENTER. Jurisdiction of Dorado Bay Police Department." Sam must have ordered it after he got home last night. I kept on walking, passed the cul de sac and kept going around the circle. My thoughts returned to the image of Urquardt drifting in the pond. The necktie certainly was a tantalizing detail. So was the bird we saw Deborah carrying from his property. When I got back to my house I looked back. The Mercedes was gone.

After showering and getting dressed, I sat down for a cup of tea, and became annoyed thinking that Sam should have called me about the bird by now. Then, convincing myself that it was best to avoid Sam until I had time to think about the strange bits and pieces, I decided to make another impromptu appearance at Deborah's house. Underneath the ultra-feminine pinks she had been wearing lately, Deborah was a clear-thinking woman. That was obvious from the way she handled the HOA board meetings. She claimed not to know much about her neighbor, but she obviously knew something about his property. She seemed to be sneaking around there after the party, probably thinking everyone was safely tucked in bed, so she clearly had a plan. I was going to find out what it was.

I was pretty surprised when she opened the door without hesitation, for the pretty blonde was not quite so pretty this morning, with deep circles and puffiness around her eyes, her hair stiff and straight, brushed back but not tied in a ponytail, her bathrobe hanging open over a tee shirt that barely covered her crotch. I couldn't help but notice her bowed legs and sagging folds inside her thighs. I had never seen her this way before. Either she was unaware of how bad she looked or didn't care. She stayed in place. She wasn't going to let me in.

"I'm packing," she said.

"When are you leaving?"

"You left the party before I made my announcement. I really need to get out of Dorado Bay today." I then remembered hearing her tell the women behind me, but it hadn't registered that she meant immediately after the party. Of course everyone else would understand this as part of the healing process after her boyfriend died. You reinvent your life to survive. I wasn't quite so sure this was her reason.

"Oh, Deborah," I said sadly, but smiling as sympathetically as I could. On impulse, I reached out with both my hands to squeeze her cold fist, and my action caused her to jump. She was nervous. I squinted into her face, and she cast her eyes downward. "Are you feeling all right?" Deborah nodded yes, then shook her head no and brought her face up, smiling weakly.

"I can't party any more. I shouldn't have had that cheap champagne Woofer brought." She twisted her mouth into a knot as if to say the whole party business is distasteful. "Woofer" was Earl Woodford, who couldn't pronounce his own name due to a denture problem.

"Oh, you learn to just pretend to drink when you become an elderly woman like like me," I advised her. Deborah laughed a little. She heaved a sigh. Then she opened the door wide enough to let me past her and gestured toward the living room. She followed and slumped into an armchair. I sat delicately on the edge of a chair close to the roses.

The petals were only just beginning to spread. I leaned forward to smell them and simultaneously glanced through a doorway to the bedroom hallway. I caught a glimpse of bright red, a fiberglass suitcase, standing on edge in the Florida room. I remembered the black Mercedes. I straightened up, then stood and stretched my arms over my head, and gradually, ballerina-style, my arms still up, tip-toed forward toward the room as if to take interest in something out the back window. Instead of a pond, there was a little wooded area that separated Deborah's property from the house on the next cul de sac. There was a path through it for access to the Bridgewater golf course. I stopped posing and walked right up to the window, put my hands up for a shade, and squinted toward woods. Deborah was waiting right behind me. When I turned she had a frightened look.

"I thought I saw something moving back there," I explained.

"Probably golf carts coming and going, early bird foursomes," Deborah offered. I followed her back to the front room, looking quickly to the right down the hall, where I could see directly into the bedroom. Several stacks of clothing were folded on the dark green, quilted bedspread, which looked like it had been hastily pulled up over rumpled sheets.

Deborah stood with her hands folded across the front of her bathrobe, as if in prayer.

"My house is a mess."

"Not so bad, considering. Get the dishwasher going and then let me take you out to lunch."

Deborah's face fell, almost imperceptibly, before she smiled and thanked me, then began to make excuses. "I can't, Sophie. There's too much yet to do before I can leave.

I have to make phone calls to the utilities."

"It's Sunday."

"Oh, right. But I think they have an automatic switch-off service."

"Please," I begged. "This is about friends. Utilities can wait. In fact, I'll do it for you tomorrow."

"I need to leave town by two o'clock. I need to get as far as…a friend's house in the Panhandle. You know how long a drive that is."

"Finish packing and I'll pick you up at twelve-thirty." With that I squeezed the woman's folded hands once more and turned abruptly so as to stop Deborah from mounting another argument. As I headed toward the front door, I let my eyes sweep over the kitchen and laundry rooms. Not one sign of a bird.

The phone was ringing as I opened my door. It was Sam. I listened to him crooning "Good Morning, Sunshine," the Sunday news program's theme song, and knew what he was after.

"I guess you want a full report on my interviews last night," I responded.

"If you're not too mad at me."

"I didn't learn much at the party – or at Deborah's this morning."

"Oh, so you're out sleuthing already. Spill it. Let me decide."

"There was no sign of the bird in her house this morning."

"What did you find out last night?"

"I'll explain later. I'm having lunch with her and then I have some things to do at the library."

"Such as?"

"I want to know more about the Apocalypse." There was a lapse. Sam was either wondering what I was talking about or was withholding information on his own investigation into that subject. "I just can't get that horrid tie out of my mind," I continued.

"Oh, that. I think I've seen one before, but it was probably in a catalog."

"Have you ever read Revelations?"

"In the Holy Bible?"

"Yes. At the very end, I believe."

"Not nice."

"Come here for dinner. Seven o'clock. You can forget the wine, but bring the Book." Now why was I so nice, I wondered as I hung up.

By the time I picked her up, Deborah was back to her old self, dressed in white slacks and sailor top. I had reserved a table at a vintage hotel restaurant just a mile and a half away, on the bay. "Quintessential Florida. So you leave feeling sentimental." Not very tactful. I wondered what, exactly, Deborah was feeling. Was she really sorry to be leaving? Was she grieving? Did she really love this Hank or Larry person who seemed now to be such a jerk? If so, why hadn't she introduced him to her Bridgewater friends? Has she been a little unsure of him all along? I waited until we were sipping our tropical teas to quiz Deborah about her plans.

"Where are you going for the vacation, or are you just going to ramble?"

"A friend of mine has a cabin in Kentucky. She said I can use it for a couple of weeks. By the way, Sophie, I need to ask a favor."

"And what is that?" I thought momentarily it might be care-taking a bird. I don't especially like birds. I associate them with my oldest and meanest aunt who lived in a cramped and, dare I say, "unfresh" apartment in the Bronx with a mostly unresponsive parrot, who reminded me of her husband, and two demanding parakeets who were very much like her kids.

"I'd like you to keep an eye on my house. If you see anything or anyone unusual, call this number and leave a message. It's my landlord." She pushed over a piece of notebook paper with a local number printed boldly over two lines.

"But how long will you be gone?"

"I'll be back – maybe in two weeks, maybe two months."

"I see," I replied, tucking the paper into my pocket. "I'll try to keep an eye on it."

"Thanks, Sophie. You are a good, good friend."

"I'm really sorry, Deborah, about your loss. But you are young and will find companionship again." When Monty had died almost two decades ago, I decided I would never remarry. But some women just couldn't imagine themselves without a man.

"Thank you." Deborah looked like she was going to say more, but didn't.

"Did – Hank have family here?" I asked.

"No. He was here by himself. Divorced years ago. He has a daughter someplace. And that brother in Philly I discovered after he died. We never talked about family. We didn't have time." She giggled uncontrollably, I suppose at the irony, but I began to wonder if Deborah should be going anywhere to be alone. The relationship must have been an intense one, maybe what they call "co-dependent."

"The cabin in Kentucky – is it a quiet place?"

"I think there are neighbors. It's in a small town in the mountains."

"Where is that?"

"Mmmm, I think the nearest town is Paducah. Excuse me. I need to use the ladies' room and then we had better get me home."

"It's around the corner in the hallway past the reception desk." I tipped my head in the right direction as Deborah removed a small zippered cosmetic bag from her large tote bag and then headed off. I was pondering the map of Kentucky in my memory. My idea of Paducah did not involve mountains. It was on a river. But what did I know?

My eyes were drawn to Deborah's open tote bag on the chair between us. Leaning over, I could see the edge of an envelope that looked like it might hold a plane ticket. It was in the interest of Deborah's well-being that I look, I told myself. I still believe it. I'm glad I did it. Keeping my eyes toward the desk that Deborah would have to pass, and my right hand tucked casually under my chin, I reached over with my left hand and lifted the envelope out by my fingertips, pulling it under the table onto my lap. I glanced down at the design on the flap. Green lettering with a spot of red. *Alitalia.* Deborah's dishonesty seemed to justify my further action. I pulled out the ticket and laid it on the table in front of my plate so I could read the details of her flight. Deborah was flying from Houston to Rome on Wednesday, 10:45 a.m. arriving the following evening. But what did that suggest?

I returned the ticket to its envelope and tucked the envelope back into Deborah's bag, then sat with my hands folded on the table, mulling over the conflicting fragments of information. Deborah said she was taking a peaceful break at a cabin in Kentucky. But the evidence showed she was traveling to Rome in just two days. She must have had the ticket yesterday, before her party. If she was going to Rome, why not mention that? It sounded exciting.

I can appreciate a woman's need to have secrets, but I can't tolerate a deliberate lie. Unless, she was planning now to drive straight through, spend one night at the cabin, and then take off from a mountaintop in a helicopter, landing at Houston by mid-morning Wednesday. Or unless she was afraid.

It was a quarter to seven when Sam pulled into my driveway with a big bunch of sweet peas from his garden and the Bible under his arm. He told me the garden was started by his mother when she came down to visit him many years ago. The next year she died, but he kept her garden going with the same plants. I was touched. And it got better. He did seem to be taking the Apocalypse seriously. He confessed that he had Purcell working on it and that the design of the tie did, indeed, look like a rendering of the four horsemen. I was relieved. I hadn't seen it that clearly. It was wet and muddy when they pulled Urquardt's body up on the bank, and the officers had directed me into the house. It was an educated guess.

After our meal ended pleasantly, Sam said, "Well, let's read the damned thing," pulling the Bible off an end table. "You asked me to bring it." A folded sheet from a yellow tablet marked the page on which appeared chapter six. Sam read with his glasses pushed down on his nose:

"And I saw when the Lamb opened one of the seals, and I heard, as it were the noise of thunder, one of the four beasts saying, Come and see. And I saw, and behold a ***white horse****: and he that sat on him had a bow; and a crown was given unto him: and he went forth conquering, and to conquer. And when he had opened the second seal, I heard the second beast say, Come and see. And there went out another* ***horse that was red****: and power was given to him that sat thereon to take peace from the earth, and that they should kill one another: and there was given unto him a great sword. And when he had opened the third seal, I heard the third beast say, Come and see. And I beheld, and lo a* ***black horse****; and he that sat on him had a pair of balances in his hand. And I heard a voice in the midst of the four beasts say, A measure of wheat for a penny, and three measures of barley for a penny; and see thou hurt not the oil and the wine. And when he had opened the fourth seal, I heard the voice of the fourth beast say, Come and see. And I looked, and behold a* ***pale horse****: and his name that sat on him was Death, and Hell followed with him. And power was given unto them over the fourth part of the earth, to kill with sword, and with hunger, and with death, and with the beasts of the earth."*

Purcell had printed on the yellow sheet: "See also chapter 19, v. 11-16." Sam turned to the tabbed page.

"Then I saw Heaven opened, and behold, a **white horse!** *He who sat upon it is called Faithful and True, and in righteousness he judges and makes war. His eyes are like a flame of fire, and on his head are many diadems; and he has a name inscribed which no one knows but himself. He is clad in a robe dipped in blood, and the name by which he is called is The Word of God. And the armies of heaven, arrayed in fine linen, white and pure, followed him on white horses. From his mouth issues a sharp sword with which to smite the nations, and he will rule them with a rod of iron; he will tread the wine press of the fury of the wrath of God the Almighty. On his robe and on his thigh he has a name inscribed, King of kings and Lord of lords."*

We both sat silently for a minute or two. The Bible was not for bedtime reading.

"It feels like Sunday," he finally said. "My head aches right below the eyebrows, just the way it did when my mother hauled me to church." He had told me once that his dad was Jewish but lapsed. His mother was a pretty fervent Methodist. Our backgrounds were similar. My mother was a lapsed Jew. I was never a churchgoer. The Bible had eluded both of us.

"Of course the Four Horsemen appear in secular contexts, even in pop culture," I reminded him.

"You think he bought the necktie at that 'Goth' shop in the mall?"

"We can't say for sure. It could have been a personal interest. Like the Frank Lloyd Wright ties for architects, or a fishing tie, or even like the Mickey Mouse and Peanuts ties that benefit Save the Children." I was nudging him toward saying something about his investigation of the tie. He didn't. I thought carefully about my next words. Then I said, "For the moment, let's assume it's not his choice."

"So, what do you have up your sleeve?" Sam lifted one eyebrow, as if to open a dare.

"I did a little reading at the library this afternoon. The critical scholars say that Revelations is not an easy text to interpret. There never has been a conclusive agreement on whether it is history or prophecy. It can be made to seem awfully dark. People have misused it."

"A warning?"

"Of some degree. Be good or the goblins will get you sort of thing – or the jaws of hell, if you believe in it."

"I don't believe in the goblins."

"So that's your excuse for . . . misbehavior?"

"I have a conscience." He tapped his right shoulder and grinned.

"You don't think that's superstition?"

"What do you believe?"

"That there are some things that are more innate than cultural to keep us on the straight and narrow." I don't know where this comes from. It's very instinctual, but I was waiting for him to say it's, to use his vocabulary, crap. He surprised me.

"I can believe that we are born *good*, and that life experience corrupts. Parents can corrupt us." Sam must have been thinking of all the criminals he had known in his lifetime. "But I don't think there are naturally good people. There's always got to be motivation. Sometimes it's fear. Sometimes it is a desire to be better than anyone else."

"You make goodness sound like a weakness," I replied.

"Well, where would it come from, then?"

"I don't know," I answered. "It's one of life's mysteries."

"The mystery is all."

"Yes, not knowing something for sure – if there is a moral and just universe – is what makes us – or me, at least – wanting to help tip the scales in that direction." At the same time my words came out I knew they weren't entirely sincere. I had a built-in sense of right and wrong, but it was probably a consequence of punishment meted out, as was the custom, with the help of a hairbrush on the behind. And by example. My mother was Jewish once upon a time. Supposedly, Yahweh spoke to her directly then. No mediator needed. In my childhood, though, the only candles in our house were for emergencies. My mother died a tired but guilt-free woman.

"I'll ask Purcell, whose Bible this is, what he thinks. He went to Sunday School," Sam said. Jim Purcell was a perk he got after his heart attack, and they both were kept so busy that they never had much time in the office together. Sam would find sticky notes on his computer screen. Bright orange or pink always meant URGENT. Blue ones were FYI. Now Sam pulled out his datebook and removed an orange one.

"He left this for me. It says: 'REV. DOCTOR CLUE CALLED 8:30 A.M. SAID IMPORTANT. I'LL BE IN AT 11 TOMORROW AFTER INTERVIEW AT CHANNEL 9.'"

"What do you make of that?" I asked.

"For one thing, Purcell is getting pretty friendly with the new Channel 9 anchor, also quite a dandy. As for the meaning, well, Reverend Clough, L.L.D., is the clergyman officiating at Urquardt's funeral. A fussy little Protestant of some splinter denomination. Probably just wants reassurance that the body will be there."

"Sam, now you are sounding bored with this case."

"Okay. Back to business," he growled. The tie – some of the symbols are pretty suggestive – the sword reminds me of the old scar across his abdomen. The robes dipped in blood – I don't know. We haven't seen any robes yet."

"What about the seals? They seem like something a secret society would have," I suggested. "Also the white robes," I added.

"You're thinking the Ku Klux Klan might be involved?"

"Not that. But something along those lines."

"Who are these horsemen? Are we supposed to be threatened by them?" Sam asked.

"War. Pestilence. Famine. Death. Everyday occurrences in ancient times."

"Ha! And now!" Sam patted the Sunday paper folded over the arm of the chair next to him.

"And then there is the fifth one, the white horse, sometimes interpreted as Christ. A Christ figure, at least. That's meant to be the hopeful part. There's a similar story in Hindu writings. At the end of the Kali Age, the god Vishnu appears as a rider on a white horse to destroy evil."

"And this idea turns up again and again in popular literature."

"Well, especially Christianized secular literature, like in the Middle Ages. The white knight on a white horse. And, you're right; we see it in movie westerns and romance novels. Maybe that's all it is, a Hollywood souvenir." I had to laugh at the possibility this might be right. We'd look like such fools. But Sam suddenly looked very sober.

"I think we're getting carried away, Sophie. We're wasting our time. Your time."

"And your money?"

"No. I wasn't thinking of that. It's just that I think – based on my own personal experience - it was just a tie somebody gave him."

"But, Sam, Roland Urquardt just wasn't the type to be

wearing that tie, even if it was a Hollywood movie depicted on it. There had to be a special reason."

"That's not solid evidence, m' dearie." I took that as admonishment.

"Well, what else do we know about Mr. Urquardt? What about the bird?"

Sam yawned and then got up to check my coffee maker. He whirled the last of the dark stuff in the pot. "Purcell grinds his morning coffee from shiny beans – Fair Trade, grown in the shade. Then he uses a press pot. Know what that is?" I nodded. "Is it too late to catch the news?" Clearly, detecting for this evening was over. And soon he left.

He hadn't asked me anything more about what I'd found. I had for some reason turned him off. He probably was thinking there he was, a toughed-assed police detective with 35 years under his belt, having this silly conversation with a librarian who had foolish romantic notions about the private eye business. But he'd be wrong. I know detecting isn't a noble calling. It is pretty damning of the human race. Was he afraid of hurting my feelings?

About an hour later, just as I was getting into bed, he phoned me.

"You won't believe what I found."

I suddenly wasn't tired.

"After I left you I ruminated over the incident and recalled what I had learned about carrier pigeons from both war novels and police training sessions. I went to my office and did a search on the World Wide Web. The color was right. I wasn't able to see markings that night, but I had a suspicion. So I copied a bit of crucial information into a new file I labeled "Urquardt: Communication." Listen to this:

These birds, Sam read, had been used as messengers during battles over at least 3,000 years. The Greeks used them to deliver news of the winners from Olympic Games. He said he remembered in New York City they were raised for racing and kept on rooftops. Like other birds, pigeons have good eyesight. They use familiar landmarks and the sun's position to guide them, also something about the magnetism of the earth.

"I don't know how far they can fly, but maybe you can find out." I quickly went to my computer and soon read what I saw to Sam: "Pigeons can fly very fast (50 miles) an hour, and in two days they can cover almost a thousand miles. Homing pigeons (Rock Doves) are a blue color with iridescent purple and green on their necks and wings. Dark gray blue line across their tails, and two dark bars over their wings. Grayish pink bills. They nest in crevices in rock cliffs or in niches, or on lofts of buildings. There was a whole lot more, even that pigeons seem to know positions of the sun and stars, and may even follow roads.

"That's good, Sophie, thanks," he said. "But there's a

caveat here." He quoted from his material: "'. . . the use of carrier pigeons did bring with it certain limitations, notably that as pigeons could only be trained to fly to known positions, e.g. base headquarters, they could therefore only be deployed from the front line to rear positions and not in the other direction unless troops were settled in a particular location for a lengthy period of time.'"

"I have to think on this." I knew Sam by now. It was like an ember in his brain. He had to poke it around some more before he could get a flame.

Suddenly I realized that, all the intellectualizing about our Internet research, I had forgotten to tell Sam that Deborah was going to Rome, and that she had lied to me. But it was now 11 o'clock. It would wait until morning. I also had forgotten to ask what the other detectives had said about a dog. And where was the watch on Urquardt's house had been the night she took the pigeon?

Monday, June 15

On my second walk around Dorado Circle the next morning, I was thinking back on little things Deborah had told me and things she hadn't. A little more questioning on my part might have yielded some leads to the purpose of the crime and the perpetrator. There probably were things those black-jacketed men had said to make it clearer whether they were friends of Roland or not. They could just as well have been enemies, the killers even. But Deborah had seemed even more evasive at lunch. She had promised to call me from Kentucky to let me know she had arrived safely. But now that I knew she was in fact headed out of the country, to Rome, on Wednesday, I really didn't expect it. If she did call, maybe on Thursday, after she arrived in Rome, what would her story be then? "Oh, I just decided I would be bored in Kentucky," or "My cousin surprised me with a birthday present"?

I wish I had asked her for a contact number, maybe her friend who owned the cabin. That might have revealed if the cabin was a total fiction. On the other hand, she didn't say her friend would be there with her. Suddenly I remembered the favor she had asked. When I got into the house and dug into my handbag I found the number – but no name. She said it was for her landlord. That meant she didn't own the house; she had no financial assets. Was she running out on the rent? I decided to make a call just to introduce myself and explain that I intended to follow up. I punched in the numbers and got an answering machine: Shady Lane Property Management. I left my name and number, but wondered if the name of the company was prophetic.

I could very well understand Deborah leaving this mess behind; she already had enough of suspicious activities in

Hank's demise. The murder of the man next door would be upsetting to any woman living alone, especially if it were a robbery, or if there were illegal activities going on. If the thugs who visited still thought she knew something, they could come back and threaten her – or worse. Still, if her neighbor had shown no interest in her socially, how would she have become involved with Urquardt? And when?

After lunch Sam called. He had some news. Jim Purcell had strolled casually into the office after his interview with a length of paper from the old FAX machine.

"He stood in front of me just watching me stroke the fur of that damned cat that wanders in and wants attention from me. Why me?" This creature, I knew from our earlier days of sharing lunch in the library garden, hung around during the day and left the building when the nine-to-fivers did, including the people who fed it. Nobody knew where it went or if it had nighttime owners.

"And then…?" I asked impatiently.

"He said the tie was custom made in Florida. There's a small supplier in Miami – or was – it recently closed shop. But we know it sold off its accounts to the parent company, some outfit in Atlanta that makes expensive gifts bearing corporate logos. You see them advertised in Sky Mall. Leather notebooks, fountain pens, and the like."

"I get the idea. Did Jim ask who requested the Four Horsemen theme?"

"He said the transferred accounts from the specialty store, as well as the information about remaining stock, have been folded into the parent company's records. The stock's just archived in categories with numbers. Nothing to describe items. No record of customers. Nobody I talked to had ever even seen what was sent from Miami. It would take a while to find out. I'm not sure it's worth it."

"There's got to be an old catalog," I suggested.

"I thought of that, too. Shredded, Purcell said. Besides, that tie could have been made to order from a drawing. Company logos, remember," he added sounding almost glad to have come to a brick wall.

"I guess detecting is partly elimination of possibilities," I offered consolingly. I think I was consoling myself. I liked the idea of that tie.

Sam had to go to Pensacola. While he was gone, the radio news reported that a husband who had been jailed on suspicion of murdering his wife and her two kids by a prior marriage hung himself. He didn't call me until 8 pm because when he returned from Pensacola he was caught up in phone conferences with the handlers who kept the media at bay. He said he didn't even think about the Urquardt case until after he found another orange sticky note on his computer screen with the note: REPORT ON MY DESK. FROM NY THIS AFTERNOON.

It was headed "Weaver, Keeble, Tucker & Thomas Profile." Urquardt's law firm. What followed was a set of biographical notes on the four principals, all of whom were expert in military law. These profiles cited their institutions of higher learning, traced the career moves of the subjects, listed the courts where they were admitted, and mentioned topics of special interest to them as individuals. There was nothing that stood out, except one unusual fact. All four had been educated abroad. In spite of their Yankee-sounding names, they were from or had lived in Bulgaria, Yugoslavia, Chile, and Germany. In 1986, all four had retired.

There was a second page, a profile of Roland Urquardt compiled in 1985. It said, essentially, that he was a solo practitioner who frequently contracted with other firms to find and investigate witnesses of crimes in other countries. He was fairly fluent in seven languages: German, Russian, Dutch, Czech, Polish, Italian, French – and of course English. In 1963 he gave a substantial amount of money to a language school in California. In 1975 he was awarded a Lifetime Achievement medal by the Military Law Task Force.

A third page was printed from a website.

"In a free and democratic society, the military protects the nation against foreign enemies and assists it domestically during emergencies.

In an oligarchy or dictatorship, the military is transformed from an institution that serves its citizens into one that controls them. Indications of problematic militarization are:

"When an inordinate percent of a nation's wealth is directed away from the citizenry and its social needs, and into a military/industrial clique that saps the wealth of the nation;

"When foreign wars and incursions serve the interests of corporate wealth, and not the national well-being;

"When participation in the military becomes an unwarranted burden, and youth are coerced, forced, and manipulated to serve in institutions that do not serve their interests;

"And, when the military itself carries such influence with political/corporate leaders that the very decision-making process of democracy is threatened.

"When these four conditions become the norm, rather than the exception, the citizenry of a country become servants to its own government. The Military Law Task Force monitors these aspects of military life and involvement, creates programs to counter unnecessary militaristic involvement, and reports its finding to the National Lawyers Guild and the nation."

"So what is this all about?" I asked. "What was the question?"

"Questions. When Jim first heard about the law firm's specialty he wanted to know more about why that was a specialty, and also why Urquardt would be involved with military law."

"Smart."

"Well, he sometimes overdoes it." Sam told me all he remembered about military law harked back to World War II and the concerns about the behavior of Navy men stationed along the east coast all the way from Maine to Florida. In those days there were enemy boats out there, and a lot of tension. Civilians, too, came under the system during the black outs and other defense procedures. Nobody went down to the beach. Nothing like martial law. "My first reaction to Purcell's document was 'What the heck does this have to do with the price of tea in China?'"

"But then?"

"Well, I still don't know what he thinks it means. I was exhausted. But when I got home I poured myself a drink and sat down in front of the TV. I fell asleep. Something woke me up. I thought it was something on the program – a shout or gunshot or something. When the cobwebs cleared I realized I had dropped a book off my lap. But I also had a flash: I saw that damned tie in my dream.

"Good for you," I said. "You busted through that brick wall, Superman." Sam raised an eyebrow. I know it was corny. He didn't deserve it.

"You a Jungian?" he asked.

"I think so," I admitted.

"I'm a Freudian," he replied grumpily.

Tuesday, June 16

Sam phoned me the next morning at nine, none the wiser about either the law practice or the tie, but he wanted to know what I was doing all day. I wanted to ask him if he'd had any further dreams, but instead I said I was going to the library and needed a few hours before I had something new for him.

"You spend more time there now than when you had a job," he said jovially.

"Enjoying it more, too," I replied, "but I feel like I'm on a deadline – no pun intended."

"What's up?"

"I'm half-expecting a call from Deborah Conyers tonight or tomorrow. She promised to get in touch when she got to the cabin in Kentucky. She didn't say when that would be, but since she's actually flying to Italy today, it could be tomorrow, after she gets settled in Rome. At least I hope so."

"Rome? What's this?"

"Oh, sorry, Sam. I keep forgetting to tell you." I explained what I had found out by looking into Deborah's handbag at lunch. I told him I knew a citizen could be a snoop even if it wasn't very nice, whereas a policeman would need a warrant.

"Don't get mad when I say this, Sophie, but I think you

are getting worked up about someone who has no bearing on the case." He spoke with such a sympathetic tone that it hurt my feelings more than if he had straight out told me to stop. In the old days I would have made no further comment and just kept things to myself, but now I decided to bulldoze ahead.

"I'm convinced she knows more about Urquardt's death than she has let on, and I'm worried that the murderer might know Deborah knows who he or she is. I also forgot to tell you I saw a black Mercedes sitting in the street early the day Deborah left."

"That could have been a friend stopping to say goodbye."

"I've never seen that particular car before."

"So the friend got a new car."

"No. It's too much like the cars she said were coming and going at Urquardt's. Someone may be watching her."

"You think someone may have followed her to the Panhandle? And to Houston? And to Rome?"

"I'd feel terrible if something happened to her, Sam. I feel responsible somehow. That's all."

"Well, there's nothing that can be done until you know where she is. Meanwhile, we gotta find something more on this dead guy."

"Is Purcell working on something?"

"He's working on the family connections and trying to

find out more about the old Urquardt house. I found out that Purcell's appearance on TV wasn't about police work, much to my relief, but about historic architecture. Jim tells me he's an amateur house historian and a collector of antiques recently, since he had inherited his aunt's Victorian cottage on Front Street. It is chock full of period furniture."

Front Street was the grandest place to live in Dorado Bay when the seaside resort town first got built up around 1900. Sam had seen it once when he had to pick Purcell up early in the morning to go to Pensacola. It actually was within walking distance of the station, in the heart of the swanky neighborhood called Old Harbor. Of course by now it had been hemmed in by newer apartment houses, stucco-on-brick, mostly built in the 1940s.

"It's on an island," according to the man who sold Urquardt fishing tackle," I told Sam.

"When did you find that out?"

"Deborah's party. He was going to show me exactly where on a map he has of the shore. Tell Jim about it. Innes Hardware." Sam harrumphed. "Are you going to go and knock on the door?"

"We can't make a move like that. Even hanging around a private island in a fishing boat would set up alarms if there is anything funny going on. "We need to find out who lives there. Officially, it's in a trust."

"You think his father can still be alive?" Oops! "I forgot

to tell you what else Arch Innes said: Roland bought some fishing tackle for his dad. I didn't ask him when."

"No living relatives have come forward. The sister died last year. She was older than he was, and from a previous marriage once removed. It's hard to explain. Let's just say it was a mixed-up family. Apparently Roland's mother remarried after she left his dad. The sister, Mary Randall, was his stepfather's child. The new marriage gave Roland a younger half-brother, but we don't have an address for him."

"What was his name?"

"We think his last name was Foucault. We don't know his first name yet."

"What was the mother's first name?"

"Geneva. There were some old letters from her in Urquardt's – Roland's – desk. Her name and address were printed on the back of the envelope. Geneva Foucault. That's why we figure the half-brother is a somebody Foucault. I wonder if you could track her more recent history."

"What about the law firm?"

"Since it closed its doors in 1986, all the partners have died. Roland wasn't a partner, but a private contractor with them. We haven't figured out his exact role."

"It closed the year before he landed here. But there must be records concerning its dissolution. There are lots of reasons to dissolve a partnership."

"As well I know," Sam said, referring to his first wife.

"Maybe they all became consultants, like Roland did."

"That's a way to go underground."

"Would Roland be consulting on matters relating to military law?" I wondered out loud. "I wasn't in Florida when submarines came. I think of dictatorships. Countries with vast armies patrolling the streets often have a corrupt ruler or a series of them. There are a few corrupt governments on islands not that far away. And we have a flow of international traffic through Miami. No doubt some mad Russians or bad sheikhs have luxury condos in Florida."

"That's just the dramatic part above ground. More than likely Urquardt moved around wherever he had to go. Your neighbor did say he was gone a lot. Maybe we should see if he owned a private jet."

I was not in the mood for the stale library genealogy room yet. If ever you want to feel young, just spend an afternoon there some day. Instead, I changed into my bird-watching outfit. Three-quarters of an hour later, I was parked at a wildlife preserve at the south tip of Siesta Key and standing alongside the car with my binoculars steadily trained on a dock attached to a spot of sand edging a very narrow private island. I had found Arch Innes in his store and he showed me exactly where to go.

At this end, there was room for one substantial house with covered verandahs. I could see the various angles of red rooftops tilted between the mangrove and the drooping fronds of the coconut palms that stood in a ring like candles on a birthday cake. This was the northern end I was watching. The only way you could get there was by a private bridge with a guard house at the mainland end, the ultimate gated community. Castles surrounded by a moat.

After fifteen minutes of no action I got back in the car, consulted my map, and pulled back onto the road connecting all the keys. I headed down the main road connecting the keys to Concha Key, turning at the side road leading to another preserve. Its parking lot was across from the southern end of the private island. To my surprise I saw the old house, built of stone with a crenellated roofline. It had a main entrance facing my way – or so it seemed, with two staircases leading up to a double door that looked like it had been looted from a Medieval fortress. Between the stairs was a tall sculpted form that might have been the centerpiece of a piazza fountain in Rome.

My high quality binoculars – bless Robin again – allowed me to see some people get out of a third black limousine that pulled up behind two others on the drive. The drive seemed to emerge from a thickly wooded area behind the house. Nothing else was visible except two narrow boxes set back on either side of the main building.

I reminded myself to ask Arch if there might be a more detailed aerial view. Otherwise, the only way to see the layout of this island was to go there by boat, despite what Sam said.

The island was positioned close to the mouth of a small inlet which extended for a block through a mainland neighborhood and then into a public park. If Sam and I drove to that park, we could ride bicycles to the streets that paralleled the Gulf. It looked, however, like the beach along that shore was all private property, homes with their own slips for launches or sailboats. If Sam didn't want to take a boat out there, our only other choice was to swim. I wondered how deep the water was.

I decided I needed to get to know Jim Purcell's brain a little better, but not until I could find out his exact address. I didn't dare ask Sam! Luckily, I knew someone else who lived on that once-fashionable street. Eve Carmona had been a friend of mine for about fifty years, going back to life in the New Jersey suburbs. Eve's husband had been a food distributor and died of a heart attack on the golf course, the victim of his own competitive nature. Andy Carmona was the first in the neighborhood to build a big barbecue pit. He was first to own color television. He was embarrassed when neither of his sons got into Yale, his alma mater, even though one went to Princeton and the other to Columbia. Andy had started to campaign for his grandson to get into Yale by insisting he go to an elite private academy known to push in that direction. But he died before he saw the boy refuse Yale when he was accepted to West Point.

Eve was very different. She wore old and repaired clothes, and rarely had her hair done professionally. She told her close friends she preferred to use her "allowance" to hunt for antiques. Her mother, until she died soon after Andy did, sent her own cleaning lady to Eve's once a week and that was the day Eve would go out on her treasure hunting expeditions. The Carmona house was a new split level like ours but furnished with good furniture, mostly from the 18th century. I asked once why they didn't buy a more appropriate house, like a Georgian manor, a showcase for the antiques. Eve said that would be inviting break-ins. She was no dummy.

"You're the only one around here who knows this stuff is worth anything," she used to tell me. I had told her my own father had owned a second-hand furniture business when we were little kids. His father, right after he immigrated, worked for an upholsterer who catered to the very wealthiest New Yorkers. When Modern was coming in, style-conscious people no longer liked their inherited pieces. Grandfather was a shrewd man. In his old age he became a rag and bone man, using a horse to pull his cart. It caught more attention than a truck would. He went through the neighborhoods where his employer's former customers lived, and those who remembered him sometimes gave him an old piece of furniture among their discards. No doubt they thought he had fallen on hard times. Grandfather took these to Father to sell to the high end dealers, and they split the profits. That's how my sisters and I learned the difference between Federal and Chippendale, and between chests made in Pennsylvania and Massachusetts.

Eve now had very little left of her collection. Her children weren't interested in them, so about ten years after Andy died she had passed most of the hoard on to her younger sister Emma and moved to an apartment with just a few favorite pieces. This sister had moved to Florida with her husband to get into the real estate business, and soon they had their own "cottage" on Front Street. Then, about fifteen years ago Emma's husband died, so Emma invited Eve to come down and the widows have since lived together, each with her own social interests.

Eve was fond of saying she enjoyed being reunited with her old furniture almost as much as being reunited with her sister. It was her job to polish their shared belongings. Even when company was there she would rub a cloth over the mahogany and bird's eye maple if she saw the tiniest amount of dust. I decided it was time to pay a visit to Eve.

It was really Emma I thought could help the most because she had been here longer. I was hoping she might remember the history of the houses in the area, including the island. But first I asked if they knew Jim Purcell.

"I don't know the name, and haven't heard that there's a policeman living in the neighborhood," Emma replied, "but there is a good-looking young man who moved into a house about a block down. We see him walking by, probably on his way to work. I guessed he was a virgin stockbroker."

"I remember the woman who lived there. She died," Eve said.

"That's right. Ann Christiansen. We watched the ambulance from the front porch," said Emma. "Too bad, I thought at the time, because she owned one of the few of these 'old ladies' that are still single family homes. Most have been broken up into apartments." But, lo and behold, she had a nephew who took it over."

"If this Jim Purcell bought it, he's got quite a job on his hands," Eve chipped in. "She wasn't keeping it up. The paint was peeling and the ivy was so thick it was pulling off the side porch!"

"The young man had it painted this summer," Emma said. They both took me out to the street and pointed to a dark green house with a turret. When we went back in and Emma offered either sherry or tea, I took the tea. I told them how nice everything looked here. The Persian carpets were worn, but I guess that's the way they are supposed to be. The antiques were gleaming and smelled like old-fashioned paste wax, not the spray-on stuff.

"I have another question," I announced. "I'm doing some research and wonder if you know anything about the family who built a house in about 1920 on that private island just off Concha Key." Concha Key, closest to Old Harbor, was right out their front door. "The owner gave paintings to the museum in the 1960s," I added.

"I remember the stories about those island people," said Emma excitedly. "They must have been quite the couple. The house was modeled after a manor house in England. They spent millions on it, unheard of in that day. The other rumor that was still afloat fifty years ago, when we arrived, is that they apparently ran into some gangland trouble when they ran a private casino. That was in the newspapers when they died in an airplane crash in 1960 or so. Apparently the place passed to a son and there hasn't been any scandal since then. I don't even know if he still lives there."

"I don't understand," I replied. "I looked in the old card catalogs for a reference to the Urquardts, and there was no mention of this article or any other."

"Urquardt? That wasn't their name. Eve, do you remember anything about this?"

"It was before my time. It didn't even know about the house out there. You can't see the island from here."

Well, that dumbfounded me. I had presumed Emma was talking about the parents of Rudolph. But maybe she was confused by local folklore. I persisted: "In the obituary, did it mention the names of Foucault?"

"It wasn't an obituary, as such, just a story. They crashed somewhere in the northeast near their summer home. Maybe it was her second husband who crashed with her. I just remember the sad ending."

I guessed the story was written by a local reporter, all sensation and few facts. I wondered if that reporter was still alive. You'd think, though, that the article would have mentioned the children if they also were known in Dorado Bay. If they weren't Urquardts who died, if they were New York Foucaults, then was the house still in the hands of Urquardts? Normally, I'd check the city directories for a name of residents at a particular address. But how does a house on a private island show up in the city directory? How would it show up in the real estate records? Sam said it belonged to a trust. If there was a transfer of title it would show up. But how old was the trust?

"What about the paintings donated by a Rudolph Urquardt? Weren't you a docent at the museum? I directed this question to Emma.

"Yes, and I have a vague memory of this, but I don't recall much fuss about it. Usually we have a special exhibit and a reception and all. I don't recall anything like that."

"Strange." I said agreeably. I still had time to work on this before I could find Jim Purcell at home. It would have to be a trip to the art museum or the library again, to track down that article. I decided to take the path of least resistance. I thanked the ladies for tea and said I promised to keep in touch, then drove my car to the small lot reserved for the museum, just a few blocks away.

It had been a Mediterranean Villa before it was an art museum, and had been expertly transformed with adjustable lighting and shades for the original skylights. Art snobs had thought the architectural expenditures out-valued the collection. Whether Rudolph Urquardt's contributions changed that balance, I didn't know, not being much of an expert myself.

The curator, Suzanne Simpson, was available, fortunately, but she was far too young to have been here when the Urquardt gifts were made. She looked in the files and found the record, including a photo like the one that appeared in the newspaper. She frowned a little, and said, "There were four, but one of them was stolen in 1986. It was the most interesting of the set, so someone knew what they were looking for." She went to another file not unlike the library's old oak card catalog, and pulled out a small box. In it were some slides. She took them over to a light table and let me stand beside her as she ran a suspended magnifying glass over them. They were very busy-looking, therefore hard for me to make out, with my trifocal vision, but she read the description:

"'Foucault, Gustav. French. Series on war. 1936-39. 1963:11-14. Four oil paintings on canvas, 18x26. Gift of Rudolph Urquardt.' Not much information. I can look up the artist, if you like."

"Can you describe what you see in them? Trifocals, you know, don't help much in viewing these."

"Oh, certainly." She pointed to the first: "This shows a group of soldiers mounted on very mean-looking horses advancing toward the center of a town. At least I presume it is the center, maybe a market center, because there's a fountain in the middle of a square and some ordinary people – see here the woman in the shawl and her children running away, and the cart of vegetables overturned. The second," she went on, moving her finger, "looks like a, well, assault on a woman in her bedroom. The sword tip is holding up what looks like rags, but it's probably her clothes, because she is nearly naked." She paused and ran her hand across her forehead. "I can understand why we haven't had this on exhibit." She then went on to the next. "This one shows a…pile of dead men, soldiers, perhaps. It looks like the square again, with the fountain dry. There are some flames at the edges of the frame. And the final one," moving the glass, "is the retreating horsemen riding outside a town that is just a lot of destroyed buildings. They are passing between fields where the grain is flattened and more bodies are strewn. That's the one that was stolen."

Her voice was sober. I held my breath. I could hear my heart beat, it was so still in the windowless room. We were in the basement of the museum and I suddenly felt suffocated. I managed a "thank you" and asked if we could go upstairs.

"Yes, the light of day would be welcome," said this young lady who was so well-mannered for her generation, and smartly dressed in a red, long-sleeved, turtle-necked sweater and an A-line, black skirt with big patch pockets, and ballerina flats.

"Is it possible I could talk with someone who was here at the time of the theft?"

"Well our director is very new, but one of the guards will remember. They've both been here the longest of anyone. Institutional memory seldom is kept at the top."

As we rode the elevator to the second floor of the museum, where one named John was on patrol, I asked where she had prepared for her career.

"I went to a girl's school in a suburb of Chicago and fell in love with art by visiting the galleries and museums with a friend who wanted to be a sculptor," she answered. "My parents insisted I do something practical – business finance. So they sent me off to The University of Michigan, but I spent my summers traveling to London, Florence, Venice, Paris, and finally convinced them I could combine the two fields. I took an MBA and also an MFA at Santa Clara in California, a small school, but one with a little museum where I was hired as a student assistant to the curator. They hired me to handle the endowment part-time, and when I took this job, because the museum is so small, I began to handle the endowment here, too. We have a big committee of volunteers." She smiled graciously, perhaps gratefully. Her talent was wasted here. I thought she wouldn't stay long. She seemed grateful for someone who actually wanted her to talk.

"This is quite a treasure you have in Suzanne," I said to the guard when she introduced me to him.

"We love her," John Bartholomew replied. She's very friendly toward the lowest of us, and she keeps us in our jobs."

"I'm here to find out more about the Urquardt bequest, and Suzanne said one of the paintings was stolen before her time, but that you might remember that event."

"Oh, yes I do," John replied, his face reddening. It occurred to me then that my question was not a tactful one. After all, he was the guard. He must have felt somewhat responsible. "It happened right before our eyes," he told me. "Some young feller said he was from the restorer's and the receptionist let him go down to the basement. About half an hour later he came up with a wrapped painting. It wasn't very big, you know. About the size of a poster. Nobody stopped him going out the door. It wasn't until about 45 minutes later when I went down to get my jacket and go home that I found our curator tied to his chair. The thief pulled a gun on him after asking to see the painting. It's a policy, you know, as a public museum, to allow people to see any of our collection."

"Yes," I said, "or I wouldn't be here." I smiled and he

reddened again.

"He signed in for the appointment made by a curator from a German museum."

This was interesting, but I changed the subject to the accession. "Do you remember when Mr. Urquardt gave the paintings to the museum?"

"Oh, yes. Our director wasn't especially thrilled to get them, but his field was modern art. He was trying to influence the direction of acquisitions. He had actually hoped to get something quite different from the Urquardt collection. It never happened." I remembered then the mention of Rudolph's personal gallery expressly for modern art.

"Too bad. These were not especially nice to look at, though. And I've never heard of the artist."

"Some relative, I think." He laughed with his chins resting on his chest and his eyebrows raised.

"Are you serious," I asked.

"That's what some people were saying at the time."

"Was there no attempt to get the painting back?"

"Very little. We weren't flush at the time so we were happy with the small payment from the insurance. The police weren't too interested in art thefts. We let him get away with it. You didn't hear that from me, though."

"What about Mr. Urquardt? Wasn't he upset?"

"He was out of the country. He wasn't exactly a regular patron and I don't know if he ever set foot in here." How odd, I thought to myself.

"Didn't you have a reception and showing of the work?

"He wouldn't let us."

Don't you find that odd – to make a donation to call everyone's attention to himself and then be unsociable?"

"It is unusual," Suzanne replied. "Most donors at least agree to appear at an opening."

"John, do you know if it was his family who built the mansion in the photo?"

"I have no idea. I'm sorry, Mrs. George."

"If Rudolph was Roland's father, it's surprising the museum didn't court Roland's interest," I thought out loud.

"Who is Roland?" Suzanne asked.

"Oh, my murdered neighbor," I answered carelessly, leaving both the curator and guard speechless.

I had until seven before I could expect to see Jim Purcell on Front Street. I decided to duck into the library and talk to one of my former colleagues. Mary Kate was free and happy to see me. I explained that I had been trying to track down information about a local art patron and after I gave her the name she went right to work on the computer and came up with the same newspaper reference I had already found.

"Mary Kate," I asked. "Do you know what newspapers we had here in the 1960s?"

"I was just a kid, then, but I can find out for you." She

went to a shelf of business directories and brought a stack to a table. "If you don't mind looking yourself, they should be in here." I had no choice but to go through them methodically and came up with two names, apparently the progenitors of our current single daily. I scribbled the two names on a scrap recycled paper they provide, using a little stubby pencil from the box, and then approached her again.

"Do we have original copies of these?" I asked.

"I'm not sure what's left after the hurricane of 1977 – our basement was flooded – but I'll find out. What years do you want?"

"Anything from January 1959 to December 1961 – if you can do it." She tried to smile, but it came across more as an unbelieving grimace. In a few minutes she was back looking happier.

"The only Dorado Bay paper before the 1980's was a weekly. I have the 1959 editions – this is half of them and Gretchen, our student intern, is bringing the rest. The early 1960 and 1961 issues must have been on the bottom. I'll get you the September through December ones."

"And how about more recent ones?" I asked, but she had already turned and was walking away fast.

The library would be open until 9 p.m. that night, but I wanted to saunter by Jim Purcell's house around seven, in hopes he would be sitting out on the front porch. If not, I would think of some excuse to call at the door. Maybe I could fake car trouble and ask to use his phone. It was now 5:30. I had about an hour or perhaps an hour and a half to peruse the newspapers.

It was tedious work, and I admit I got sidetracked looking at the prices in the ads. Those were the days. At about quarter to seven I was ready to give up, but Marianne had brought a handful of the surviving 1962 newspapers which by then had combined and become a bi-weekly. They had added national news to the local gossip. The article I found fell somewhere in-between. The dateline was New York, September 4, 1962,

Captain and Mrs. Gustav Foucault died tragically on Sunday night when their small plane crashed and exploded in a primitive area of Canada as they were returning to their New Jersey home from a fishing trip. Mrs. Foucault, maiden name Eve (Geneva) Trandescant, still owned a winter home in Dorado Bay.

The Foucaults are survived by four living children, two by her first marriage to Otto Urquardt, Rudolph, 38, and Roland, 36; and Gustav Foucault, III, their son who is 17. A daughter survives from Foucault's first marriage, to Mary Wild. Katherine Foucault Randall, 51, lives in New York City. Gustav and Mary lost two sons in World War II, Yves and Jacques. They were 19 and 21. Mary died in 1944.

Foucault and his second wife had been friends since childhood. Their parents were partners in an art dealership in Paris. Eve had married Urquardt in 1938 but Otto divorced her in 1945. She and Foucault

married later that year.

The home in Dorado Bay was built by the Transdescants in 1922 but they used it solely to loan to clients and friends. They also died in the war.

The information was a little garbled just like it is in the current local paper, but it made clear that Rudolph was not Roland's father, but his brother, presumably the one who worked for the family business until he died of a heart attack. The story also revealed a third brother – a half-brother – who might come forward to claim Roland Urquardt's body if her were informed about the murder. He was a much younger half-brother. Possibly, he hadn't stayed in touch with Roland. I jotted down a note to myself to tell Sam about Gustav Foucault. It was another thread.

Only later did it occur to me that, if the house on the island had been owned by Geneva up to her death, then it now belonged to her remaining heir, the elusive Gustav III. Where was he? I gasped. What was her former husband doing there? Or was Arch Innes mistaken about what Roland had told him?

I parked my car halfway between the sisters' house and Jim's and started walking along the sidewalk to the dark green house. I was really tired after so much intense research. Fortunately, Jim was sitting on his porch, and I stopped in my tracks and did my best to look surprised.

"Jim! Is this where you live? How are you?"

"Tired, but otherwise great," he said. "This was my aunt's house. What are you doing in this part of town?"

"Oh, I have some friends who live on the street. I was just curious enough about the old neighborhood to want to walk as far as the beach and back again. Usually I walk around Dorado Circle in the evening, and it gets pretty boring. Your house is really quite a remarkable place! It is yours, isn't it? I think Sam told me you had just moved."

"About a year ago. My aunt left it to me in her will."

"How old is it?"

"1910. 'The Queen of St. Luce Avenue,' according to an architectural guide book of the 1920s. I'm afraid time has reduced it to something more like a duchess."

Momentarily, I thought about Duchess Deborah, who didn't have a home anymore. This house must have plenty of extra bedrooms.

The narrow three-story structure with its two-story porch had recently been painted a rather dark green with pinkish white trim (Conch Shell Alabaster, to be exact, I'd soon find out). I thought blue-black trim would look better, but to each his own.

"Sam said you've become quite an expert on old homes in the area."

"My aunt's father was an architect, so there were lots of

books in the house. Besides, there's a lot of restoration work to do. I sort of fell into it, you might say."

"Do you happen to have come across anything in that book about the Urquardt house – so-called – the one built in 1922 on the private island just across on the other side of Concha Key? It was probably called something else in the 1920s. The people who built it, I just found out, were French and named Trandescant. The daughter married Otto Urquardt, Roland's father, and they lived here. When they divorced she and her new husband, named Gustav Foucault, may have used the house, but they apparently allowed Rudolph to live in it."

"Sam gave me the house history assignment. I found it. Let's go in and look."

Jim seemed much more like a young professor than a policeman. I wondered how he got into Sam's line of work. But I didn't want to get him off track. His fingers slid over the spines of books on a particular shelf, second one up, in a built-in bookcase under a window that faced the neighbors through mounds of bougainvillea.

He found the book and searched the index and paged through to where the Trandescant-Urquardt-Foucault house was not only mentioned, but pictured, and the floor plan was included.

He offered me a glass of wine and at first I resisted, but when he told me it was from his aunt's cellar, and could be good or bad, I said I'd experiment with him. It was a sweet, gooey substance but I kind of liked the idea of drinking old wine. Pretty soon we were talking like longtime friends, even, perhaps, like mother and son. Jim was much more forthcoming about his personal thoughts than Robin ever is. I attributed it to his feminine side. Sam later lectured to me on stereotyping gays, and I argued that we all have male and female characteristics of personality, but I still think Jim was exceptionally emotionally tuned in compared to most men I have known.

I could tell he felt lashed by Captain Samuels' impatience. He said he didn't think of himself as a particularly thin-skinned person, but maybe he was after all. He was at that age when doors should be opening to get ahead in a career, and yet he felt like Sam's errand boy. If only he could be out in the field more instead of in the background, he'd be thrilled to bits, even if it were dangerous. Then he admitted that being involved at a crime scene would give him a reason to be in more frequent contact with his TV friend, Dan. Any small town journalist, even one who was leery of dating a police detective, would like to have an exclusive crime story.

I reminded him that he was already involved in a real crime, and congratulated him on his good work finding the source of the tie.

"The whole tie thing seems absurd," he said. It was my

turn to be red-faced. "It is too elaborate an idea for what seems to be an ordinary Mafia killing. It smacks of evil Boy Scouts," he went on, pulling the rug from under my feet. On the chance it had been an overly zealous religious group, Jim was looking at the organizations that had held meetings in Dorado Bay or nearby in the last two years.

I changed the subject to the furnishings of his house. He liked a couple of hand-painted, kerosene, parlor lamps sitting on a breakfront, no doubt for hurricane season, but decided they had to go. Maybe he would use them to set up a safe haven in the basement of the house. The hurricane seasons had been pretty brutal lately. There were a couple of Morris chairs upstairs that he didn't want any more – they were too late for the 1880s-1900 Aesthetic Movement style he had selected for his main rooms. There also was an iron bed in the carriage house at the back of the property. I was thinking I should introduce him to Eve until he started going on about vintage furnaces.

"I'm reading this fascinating book that has got me quite familiar with my cellar," he said, shoving it into my hands. *Furnaces for the Sunshine State, A History.* These days, having settled the AC versus fan issue, he was left wondering what to do with the monster furnace, which must be 100 years old. Well, not that old. He didn't know how old. He was too young to remember one like it, with its rotund shape and huge, muscular "arms" that reached octopus-like to all rooms of the house. He wasn't sure of the safety of such a thing, though he thought the register grills with their brass curlicue designs were attractive. He asked if I knew a way to remove the spots of rust.

"This book was written in 1955 by an engineer who no doubt thought he was writing the bible on heating systems. Within an hour of starting chapter two I knew that what he had written was something bigger. It's great reading for its history of ideas. I hadn't thought of it before, but central heating was hardly as important in Florida as it was in Pennsylvania or New York. Interest grew after the flu epidemic of 1918." He read:

"In the 19th century, a coal fire was used because it burned hot and long, for up to 10 hours on a load if the householder knew how to properly start the fire and spread the coals so that the air could enter from below. It was a luxury, in spite of the hard work it took to "keep the home fires burning" . . .

Jim stopped reading to tell me his mother's story: In her early marriage, left alone when his father was always on the road, she had to go down into the dirt-floor basement of the first house they rented and put pennies in the gas meter. That was bad enough. He couldn't imagine shoveling coal like his mother had done.

I was feeling anxious to get home, but he insisted on reading from the book again:

". . . Wealthy people might have servants just to take care of this

chore and a few other dirty tasks that were part of the routine in those days. In the early days of the 20th century, home heating developed rapidly. The cause was the Spanish Influenza pandemic of 1918-19 that killed 50 million people in the worst disaster in human history. In America, Ladies Home Journal *coined a new name for the room in which people received visitors, then known as 'the parlor;' it became the 'living room.' For survivors, the parlor had taken on such a sadness they wanted to forget it was where they laid out their dead.*

"That's something to ponder," I managed to comment sincerely. It must have been a Christian practice, I thought to myself.

That's not all," Jim replied: "During the summer of 1919, no one was allowed out on the street unless they were wearing a surgical mask. The virus was airborne, and people were afraid of the air in their homes, so they opened the windows to get fresh air. This increased the demands on central heating. After 1920, the Fresh Air Movement required boilers and radiators large enough to heat the building on the coldest days with the windows open."

Jim seemed awfully young to me, but he was fascinating and enthusiastic. So when he said, "C'mon down," and plucked some gloves and a flashlight out of a drawer, I followed him. He opened a door in the hallway and we peered down at a narrow wooden staircase. The single light bulb over the steps at the top was augmented by one at the bottom. From there it was a gloomy path through mildewed cartons which he told me he had not yet explored. In addition, all the gardening implements seem to have been left down here: shovels, spades, picks, and so forth. He found a lantern with dead batteries. It looked to be something carried by the patrolmen inspecting during the frequent World War II blackouts.

"Solid cement," he said, stomping his foot on the floor. "Mother would have loved this." He grinned, and I couldn't help laugh a little.

The furnace stood in the center of the basement, but two sides were blocked from view by the rotting frame of coal bins, or at least that's what he thought they might be. The coal chute was off a foot or two from one of them. There seemed to be nothing to use to direct delivered coal quite on the mark, but it smelled like coal still. He walked around the other parts admiring the girth and the surprisingly good condition it was in. Now he wanted to find the date of the contraption. It should have a patent, or at least the name of a company, which he could look up at the library. Maybe I would help him find it, he suggested cheerfully. But there was nothing obvious, no brass plate with all the information he wanted. He even ran his gloved hand around the side in case. The heavy square but convex door screeched as he opened it. There was a cavern, a wide space, lit from openings near the top of the thing, and with light gray dust thick to about a foot beneath the door opening. He could not see anything but a number on the inside of the door. He then reached over to run his hand along the wall, again hoping for raised lettering of some kind. He stopped when he touched a piece of rough cloth sticking out of the ashes. There was a metal fastener on the end of what looked like a strap of canvas overall. We looked at each other and I could almost hear him thinking what I was thinking: Let's get out of here.

"We know about when the tie was made," Sam said when he called.

"Good! How did you find out "

"Calls to old employees. The Miami outfit was named Custom Premiums. They were in business from the early 1960s to the late 1980s. Someone apparently requested that pattern in the 1970s. We haven't figured out who yet. Nobody remembers. It never became one of the standard patterns."

"You mean that it was private and exclusive?"

"Apparently. Thing is, the company usually fulfills an order by the dozens. Say a corporation is having their annual picnic. They get 250 tee-shirts made with words on 'em for the occasion. Or Frisbees with a fraternity logo."

"So the tie was not one that could be requested by anyone else?"

"Seems so. It could be ordered only by one customer

with odd taste."

"Was it just one order? A conference maybe? Like academic historians getting together to compare notes on the apocalypse? Or a religious group?"

"Purcell's working on the last you mentioned." I didn't want him to know yet that I had talked to Jim. He had seemed somewhat disdainful. Then a new idea came to me.

"Sam, what about war, pestilence, famine and death? War, especially. Military group. As in military law."

"Well! That would be a possibility. Or it could be a pest control or an agricultural corporation."

I didn't know if he was pulling my leg or not.

"Or morticians."

He was.

"Sophie, you are making me dream about that damned tie! I had another one last night."

"What was it? Do you remember anything this time?"

"Surprisingly, quite a bit. It was on a body in the morgue."

"Well, that sounds like a replay of the crime. Anything else?"

"It's so hard to remember the details, but it made quite an impression on me. I still feel it in my gut."

My skin began to prickle.

"Do you think it was really a dream? Could you be remembering an event?"

"It was one of those butterfly thoughts I get sometimes waking up."

"Those are sometimes fragments of a dream. I have them, too. Can you try to remember more, the circumstances – in the dream, or whatever it was? Were you alone when you saw the tie?" I heard him sigh.

"I can't tell you any more. There just isn't enough stuff. And I don't have time. It was more like a puff of atmosphere. Comes out of a dream spray can. It's not anything I can picture."

"But so do real memories dissipate like that, Sam. You can work on remembering, though. Let me help. I know lots of exercises for recall. I practice all the time. Senior moments, you know. We all have them"

"I told you I don't have time."

"Are you on your way out at this hour?"

"No, but I want to watch the news.

"You have ten whole minutes. Close your eyes and concentrate."

"I can see a dark room, like a cave."

"Is it the room in the police morgue?"

"No. It's too dark. And it doesn't stink."

"Any sounds?"

"Yeah. Music. I hear organ music. But it's not church music. More like classical. Or the kind you hear in elevators."

"From speakers. Not a church then. At least – well, who

knows? A memorial service maybe?"

"Maybe. Actually, I think I smelled flowers. I never knew we could smell in dreams until just now. Holy Toledo!

"I don't think I have a sense of smell when I dream. You're a good dreamer," I said to encourage him. It was true. I don't dream smells. Odd, isn't it, I thought, because we're told that it is smells our memories retain longest.

"Yeah." Sam snorted. "I recall my youthful dreams. They are in ruins all around me. What am I doing now? Confessing on a couch? You're not even a psychologist!"

I decided to ignore this. I continued to probe in the couple minutes before he was sure to cut me off.

"What was he – the corpse – wearing besides the tie? What was the fashion that year, the era?" I was seated on the bamboo ottoman, holding a stenographer's tablet on my knees. I imagined Sam lying on the couch.

"Fashion? A black suit, of course." There was an irritating long pause and then he almost shouted: "No. Not a suit. It was a black sports coat. He always wore sports coats."

"He?"

"I mean it was Andy - Andy Marcinak's funeral! It was just before the department hoo haw last New Year's Eve."

"And Andy was wearing one of those ties?"

"No. The tie was on someone else, someone in the line. Now I remember noticing the tie, but maybe not the face. I didn't speak to that person."

"Was there a guest book?"

"Yes. There was. I can get it. I know the family pretty well." Sam sounded excited. "I'm giving you a toast," he said. Then he slurped, no doubt from his bourbon nightcap.

"Here's to you, Captain Samuels," I said lifting my empty teacup. "Dreams are good." I heard what sounded like a crash, like glass breaking, but then I realized he'd carried the phone to the kitchen and was putting ice cubes in his glass for another one.

Wednesday, June 17

I had a headache when I woke up and attributed it to the weather warning. When we lived on the water I frequently had sinus problems just before a fierce storm. A fellow librarian who had knee replacement surgery told me that her knees "sang" before a thunderstorm. Something about the titanium.

Titanium, Titanic, boat. My thought process was making leaps again. Had anyone determined whether or not Urquardt, the big sea fisherman, ever owned a boat? Deborah had mentioned seeing him on a fishing yacht, but perhaps he had his own, and perhaps someone at the marina could tell them more about his activities when away from his home port, such as where he went sailing. I had the urge to call

Sam and ask, but did not want to tie up my phone. I still hoped Deborah would live up to her promise to call me to-night or tomorrow, wherever she was. What would the time zone difference be, if she were in Rome? I then connected with an earlier thought that had slipped through the cracks: get a mobile phone. Robin had been trying to persuade me to get one from the time they were first available, but I was not sure I wanted to always be reachable.

"Mum, what if something serious happened to one of us? What if you were out on the highway someplace and blew a tire? Or what if I was in an accident and no one could find you?"

"Florida state patrolmen are very good," I had replied. "They not only come to the aid of travelers in distress, but they also can spot license plates." I could hear his frustra-tion. We had reversed roles in the last few years. Now he hovered, or at least he tried. Thank goodness we live about as far away from one another as we can and still be in the same country. Mail took four or more days. I'm glad I wrote before I found Urquardt floating in the pond. If I told him about this, he'd be nagging me to move into the penthouse of a retirement home 30 stories high.

At mid-morning, afraid to miss her call, I still had not budged out of the house, even to walk around Dorado Circle. I began to mentally organize my questions for Deborah and my responses to questions Deborah might ask. Deborah would wonder if I had seen anyone around her house or Roland's, or if the police were looking for her. I wanted to ask why she had insisted that she was going to Kentucky when she actually was going to Rome? And why Rome? On the other hand, maybe I should go along with the pretense of Kentucky and see if Deborah could sustain the fiction; I could ask her what the weather was like in Kentucky, and the route to the cabin, things that would trip her up. I suspected she could not answer such questions unless someone else was telling her what to say. And who would that someone be, the generous friend of hers, or one of the black-jacketed thugs? Then I wondered how I would know if she really was calling from Rome? Should I ask Sam if there was a way they could check where she was calling from? Already he had shown sufficient disdain for my believing Deborah was somehow involved in the murder. He wouldn't help me. If she were in Rome, I wondered, could I tell by background noises, little red cars outside the hotel window honking at each other? Would she then claim they were wild geese in the neighboring Kentucky swamp?

The most troubling theory that flitted through my mind was that Deborah was being held against her will. It was imperative that I find out. What sentence construction could I use to get Deborah to make a slip, or to give me a hint?

And what if she didn't call? Then what? In which direction, which state, which country, should we begin to search for her? We?

That's when I realized in my heart that I would have to search for her alone.

"Just about everybody's dead," Sam said gloomily when he called me after lunch time. "I have run a check on every male in the Marcinak funeral guest book. On the bright side, one of them, a Frank Dobbs, committed suicide the next day. The family remembered. I guess the family kind of wondered. . . We're following that lead. His body was found on a vintage yacht moored at the public marina — with a rope around his neck."

"Hanged? How terrible!" I responded. "Was it suicide?"

"We couldn't find fingerprints, signs of struggle, or know if anything was taken. He was from Ireland. Nobody, including his wife, seemed to know why he was in Dorado Bay, Florida. The only hint of something unnatural was that he was dressed for sailing, except that a necktie was rolled up in the pocket of his windbreaker. It's in a box in the archives with his other clothes and accessories. I sent Purcell to dig it out. It's a long shot, but it could be the tie he wore to the funeral, the one I saw."

As we were talking Purcell apparently had returned, because Sam turned away from the phone, shouted "Great!"

triumphantly, and turned back to tell me: "It's a match!"

Sam now was having Purcell go back to checking on military conferences while he waited all afternoon for a report from the parent company on the Florida customers of the premium division in the last 20 years, plus a list of the customers in the Tampa Bay/Dorado Bay area.

"I didn't want to bother you," Sam claimed when he stopped by to check progress at the pond and had not come to my door first. I was standing, as I often now did, watching through my patio doors. I spotted him wandering at the edge of the pond, stepped outside and hailed him. He had trudged up the slope through the tall plants and stood dripping muddy water on my doormat, looking like a dirty dog.

"Anything new?" I asked. "I'm feeling cooped up here and they don't talk to me." In fact, my impression was they were avoiding me at all costs.

"Almost a week's gone by," he acknowledged, "and we're as stumped as we were the day he was found."

I noted that he didn't say, "the day *you* found him," but I didn't want to get into what he would call a feminist fit. I needed to focus un-emotionally on what I knew or suspected. As a matter of fact, I was fighting my own frustration for my own failure to have come to a better conclusion by now – and a simpler one.

"Sit and have a drink." I poured him a Wild Turkey straight in a sturdy lead crystal glass and made myself a light gin and tonic. He had taken his shoes off so we could sit in the Florida room as the daylight was fading and there was nothing much to watch.

"The yacht Dobbs was found on had no owner."

"How can that be?"

"It wasn't registered and nobody recognized it."

"Who was asked?"

"The neighboring boat owners and people who worked at the marina."

"So it just sailed as if from the past into an empty slip and somebody attacked him? Maybe it was the person whose slip it was. You know how long some people have waited for a place down there."

"That's silly, Sophie. You can do better than that."

"I can. Had anyone noticed that boat on the Gulf before? Wouldn't it be noticeable? I someone saw it, we could at least begin to guess what direction he came from."

"For all we know, he could have been sailing in circles. The boat was a nice one, but pretty beaten up, like it had been in a storm. It was old. Almost an antique."

A light bulb lit up my mind.

"Could it have belonged to the island estate?"

"That's a hare-brained notion," Sam declared. But then he followed with "hmmm." He said, "I don't know if anyone checked if anyone was there at the time this happened. There was no obvious connection. We couldn't check everybody who lived on water."

"It wouldn't matter if someone was there as long as someone knew the boat was there, maybe in dry dock. Maybe they intended to restore it, or just keep it for its sentimental value."

"It's a thought. We'll put it in the hopper."

"Well, now. What else can we discover?" I admit I was pretty pleased with myself for that one after a very dull day. Sam shook his head.

"There's more bad news. I've not heard anything from the company about the Florida orders for ties. Maybe I never will. Or maybe I'll get a contact name, that's all. Maybe that person is dead, too." He was looking moodily into his glass, his legs stretched out side by side, balanced on his heels. Noticing his socks were worn thin where the shoe rubs I realized how male he was, and felt very heavy-hearted, suddenly. I remembered doing laundry for my husband. I loved Monty but didn't miss that part of marriage. It was almost as stupifying as waiting for Deborah to call.

I studied Sam's face for a few moments. He still didn't get it. He wasn't really interested in my theories. It was time to be bold.

"Sam, this is really important. Listen: Suppose Roland belonged to a group of men – a clan of sorts – who performed elaborate, ritual crimes. Murders, rather. Human sacrifices. Maybe they were avengers. The Apocalypse ties are their – well, club tie." Sam raised an eyebrow.

"Wait a minute. How do we get from two murdered men to a group of murderers?"

"I don't know. I was just thinking we might look for more instances of Apocalypse ties on corpses."

"But if the murderers are wearing these ties to show they belong to the group, how is it that the victims are also wearing the ties? Are they gang members killing their own members?" Then he slapped himself up the side of the head. "Oh, I think I get it. Signature ties." I nodded and continued with mounting excitement.

"Remember I said Roland never wore ties – at least not in the neighborhood? Not even to parties."

"Yeah. So you think somebody put it on him? The killer leaves a message, a tag, so to speak, the apocalypse tie? But what about Frank, the guy I saw at the funeral?"

"I thought you said you saw the tie on one of the guests – and that Frank was found dead later with the same tie in his pocket."

"I did."

"How do you know he and the guest were the same man?"

"Yeah. That's right. I saw the tie, not the face, in the line. Maybe that guy wore that tie because he intended to tie it on

Frank when he had killed him."

"The killer may not have even signed the guest book." Sam threw up his hands. This was getting more and more complicated.

"Frank could have been in line wearing the tie and later rolled it into his pocket. A lot of men do that, don't they? They take a tie off to be more comfortable?" I paused as I had another thought. "Do you think Frank could have meant to put it in Andy's coffin?"

"You're suggesting our fellow Marcinak must have been involved, too."

"He was a police detective, wasn't he?"

"Yes."

"Well, find out what he was investigating at the time of his death."

"He died of a heart attack." I thought to myself that there are ways to make people have heart attacks. But never mind. "Maybe Dobbs was a killer but his victim got him first," Sam added. "We'll never know."

"Don't you think all of this sounds like gang work?" I suggested.

"Or a gang splitting up." He got up to leave. It was ten o'clock, my usual bedtime.

"I wish you could find out what Dobb's relationship to Detective Marcinak was, why he might be at the funeral home," I said as we parted.

"It's not that important," Sam replied, rather carelessly, I thought.

I had given up ever hearing from Deborah again and so went to bed with a coffee table book of photos of historic Florida that Jim Purcell had insisted I borrow. When the phone on my desk did ring, I was dozing with the light still on. The book slipped from my lap. As I reached over to grab it I nearly fell out of bed. I caught it and the bedpost but missed the fourth ring. Surely it was Robin, the only person in my life who would dare call me this late. A dozen ideas of what was wrong flashed through my mind before I remembered the letter I'd sent him. No doubt he'd received it and rehearsed his response. It was unfair of him to catch me off guard, half asleep. By the time my mind raced through all that, my answering machine was recording the caller's voice. It was Deborah after all.

"Sophie, I think I had better tell you what's happening," she was saying as I grabbed the receiver. Her voice sounded tiny, like a child's, and her sentences were punctuated with little gasping breaths.

"I'm here. I'm here," I responded, simultaneously pushing the button that Sam had showed me would record the conversation. I hoped the click was not obvious on the other end. "I've been waiting to hear from you. Are you calling from Italy?"

"How did you know that's where I was going?"

"*Was* going? Never mind. Tell me what's going on."

"I had to leave Dorado Bay quickly – as you might have guessed."

"I did wonder why."

"My plans changed late in the morning, before the party." Deborah had given instructions to the young woman she had hired to clean the house to arrange the flowers and then sat at the little French desk in her Florida room checking of her list of things to do before the party. The cleaning girl came to her with an envelope she had found in the third box of long-stemmed roses.

"Of course I thought it was the bill," Deborah said, "but instead it was a plane ticket to Rome. Clipped to it was a pencil written note in capital letters: "USE THIS. AVENTINO HOTEL." That was all that was on the quarter sheet of paper with torn edges."

"Did you save the note?" I asked.

"I don't remember. I could have stuck it in the drawer, or I could have tossed it in my wastebasket. It scared me to death! Someone obviously had been watching my every move, including my stop at the florist's. Someone had somehow talked the florist or driver of the delivery truck into letting him or her insert this envelope in the wrappings."

"That would be unnerving. But who would be watching

you, those same men?"

"I don't know. But then I thought: This was the miracle I needed. Now I really could get out of here, and far. The only odd thing was that I was to get on the airplane in Houston, not Tampa. I had to drive like a bat out of hell." Precisely, I thought.

"And then what happened?" As the words came out of my mouth I realized what the background noises were; planes were taking off. She was still in the airport in Houston.

"Two men met me at the airport. They were right there as soon as I parked my car."

"They must have been following you. What did they do?"

"They took me by my arms and guided me to their car and put me in the back seat. One drove us to another parking garage while the other told me our plans had changed, that the trip to Rome would come later, and that we were going to California." Her voice sounded very shaky. "He said I needed protection because of what happened to Roland, but that's all he would tell me."

"I gather these were not the same men who made the deal with you to watch Urquardt's house."

"No. These men were very ordinary looking and nice." She stopped there and blew her nose.

"Have they names?" I asked, a little sarcastically I realized.

"Joe and Tony." Of course. They were Italians without

the smelly black jackets.

"Last names?" I guess she shook her head because I couldn't hear the answer.

"So these two men, whom you know only by first name, did what next?"

"They took me to a hotel by the airport and got me a room. They stayed in the rooms next to mine, one on either side. They left the doors open but never bothered me. They used room service for food. I watched TV until I fell asleep and then morning came. We all went to the airport, to the ticket counter and got checked in on a flight to Los Angeles."

"What airline?"

"Continental."

"Flight number? Time of departure?"

"I don't remember. One of them held the tickets." Of course. And probably there were a hundred flights between the two cities each day.

"How did you get away from them to call me?"

"We just landed and I told them I had to go to the ladies. They're waiting for my bags. So that's all I can tell you for now, but I just wanted you to know. I promise to call after we get to this place they said we were going to stay."

"It is very wise to keep in touch with me," I said firmly, when I wanted really to shake her. What wouldn't this woman do as long as the men ordering her around looked like rescuers to her? I suspected one was right there listening in and she didn't even know it. I contained my anger. I wanted to ask her the other burning question

"And, by the way, what did you do with the bird?"

There was silence on the line, and then again the nose being blown gently before she answered with her question. "How did you know?"

"I was outside with Captain Samuels watching when you went around to the back of the Urquardt house. What is the story behind the bird?"

"Roland had asked me to take the bird if he …if anything was going to keep him away for a while."

"But where is it now?"

"I gave it to a friend of his." Silence. Too long.

"*Who?*"

"It was a Lewis or maybe Lewes. Oh, I can't remember anything anymore." She was talking too fast.

"It was just last week," I reminded her.

"I didn't know him. His name and number were on the cage. I just called him and said to come over right away because I was going away."

"What did *this* man look like? Black leather jacket?" I was losing faith in Deborah. The woman was much too needy to be trusted. Probably this whole thing was made up to dramatize her life – or to cover something up. But I still didn't think she could have murdered Roland.

"No." Deborah giggled in spite of her tears. "Just a tan sweatshirt. He wore a black baseball cap. Sunglasses."

"And his car? Was it a black Mercedes?" Deborah didn't answer right away.

"It was a dark green pickup truck."

"Was there a name painted on the side of the truck?"

"No, you're right; it was a black Mercedes. Honest. I'm not making this up."

"Where is the cage?"

"I left it where it was in the shed on the back of his lot. It was too big to carry and Roland showed me that the bird was tame. He wouldn't fly away without being instructed." This was interesting, I thought. Apparently she'd been invited into the backyard of this unfriendly neighbor's house.

"Was it a carrier pigeon?"

"A what?"

"A pigeon that carries messages for people."

"I don't know. It had an I.D. bracelet on one leg."

"I'll go get the name off the cage. Okay with you? I asked.

"But the name's not there any more. Roland told me to rip it off – it was on a tag with the phone number – so I could have it to call, but he told me I could throw it away."

"Did he ask you to throw it away?"

"Yes."

"*When* did Roland tell you to give the bird to this person?"

"He mentioned it a long time ago. He said, 'Deborah, you seem like someone I can count on. If ever something happens to me, I would like you to do me a favor.' And then he told me about Archie. Of course I said I would take care of it."

"But he definitely wanted the bird – Archie – given over to this particular man?"

"Yes. But I didn't think it would happen this way. The murder – when it happened I almost forgot about the bird, I was so upset."

"You're sure you can't remember the friend's name? Did you keep the phone number?"

"Nothing. Nothing, nothing, nothing. I have to hang up now." Deborah was almost screeching, in a whispery sort of way. I just listened for a few moments, then spoke slowly and firmly, more like a stern parent or teacher than a counseling psychologist.

"I'm sorry I'm so rough, but please pull yourself together. I can't help you unless you tell me what's really going on! You said you hardly knew Roland, he rebuffed you, and yet he asked you to do something this important. And it doesn't make a lot of sense." I held my breath because reason was sliding away again with impatient anger filling the void. This silly woman was in danger. Did she even know it?

"I should have known the black leather jackets were trouble," Deborah was saying, apparently reading my mind. "I should have called the police. But I couldn't because they already paid me five hundred dollars, and I spent it, and I had to keep watch on the house to earn it. But when Mr. Urquardt was killed. . . "

"You got a better offer." When I pictured the blonde woman as she had looked at the last neighborhood council meeting – a navy blazer, brass buttons, all business – I couldn't believe Deborah would be dumb enough to get herself in this tangled mess.

"Deborah, you knew that money was tainted."

"I needed the money, Sophie. Bad. I've been almost broke for about a year and a half. I never really had much. My husband didn't have a lot of life insurance way back then. We were newlyweds when he was in an accident. And then my friend Hank – he was supposed to leave me comfortable, and he didn't. He didn't even have it for himself."

I listened to Deborah repeat her excuses and thought: It was the old, old story. It was, in fact, a Florida classic. If I'd known her better sooner, I could have warned Deborah about men who drive flashy cars when they are over 65. Even black ones.

"Well, I'm sorry about your disappointments, Deborah, but you have to cooperate with the investigators now, and since you didn't exactly tell the truth it won't be pleasant."

"I didn't exactly lie."

"Come home."

"I can't. I'll be all right once I get to Rome."

"Funny you should agree to go to Italy when you think your enemies are Italians."

"Not all Italians are bad."

I quickly read between the lines. Maybe the men with her now really were Italians. Joe and Tony Gallo or Mondavi, perhaps? Maybe they had nicer after shave lotion.

"Is someone going to Italy with you?" There was a long silence, except for little hiccup-y breathy noises. Then Deborah blew her nose.

"I'll be with a friend."

The meaning of "friend" changes with circumstances, I observed silently. Someone you wouldn't even walk around the block with suddenly becomes an avenue of escape. Deborah was saying, "I'm sorry, I'm sorry…"

"And when are you leaving to go abroad?" I managed to ask.

"I don't know for sure, but I think next Wednesday." That was good. Four more working days, Thursday, Friday, Monday, Tuesday – and the weekend in between to get Sam to do something about police protection.

"Listen to me! Where will you be staying until next Wednesday?"

"I'll be in a safe place." She hung up.

Thursday, June 18

I had a sleepless night, but I walked Dorado Circle one extra time for penance. I hadn't been paying attention to my own health these days. Maybe, too, walking would vent my anger, which wasn't really fair. For the first time, I realized that being a detective was not just brain work. If friends were involved, it could give the emotions a real workout. Not that I ever felt especially close to Deborah Conyers, but I had not known much about her personal life until Urquardt's horrible death and that night when she came over and drank gin and poured out her life story. It seemed that the woman had endured more than her share of pain and loss. Now, just as she was trying to start a new life, she could be in grave danger. But she also seemed unstable.

When I got home there was a light blinking on my telephone – a message.

"It's me. We're in Pasadena. But I am calling mainly because I forgot to tell you something else I remembered about the black jackets." My ears pricked up. "Those men who offered me money belong to a war club or something. While I was getting a pencil and paper to write down their instructions, I heard them talking about their 'war games.' It sounded like they go out in the woods and play at being soldiers. They shoot at each other. They go to someone's house on the beach." Then she whispered: "I'll call you again if it's possible." Deborah had abruptly hung up. This time the call would be traceable.

I hit the button where I stored Sam's home number. He answered groggily, but listened without interrupting as I repeated the things Deborah had told me over the phone in person and then her message this morning. He grunted when I said Deborah was in Pasadena.

"Could have predicted that. It's perfect for her. I can't imagine her landing in someplace like, say, Scranton."

"I wish I had started doubting her when she said she was going to the friend's cabin in Kentucky," I said, "I was too soft, too comforting, too…" My words ran out but I think I got the point across to Sam that I knew I hadn't earned an A+ on the job.

"I told you she was ditsy. She's not in danger, she's deranged."

"I wish I had been here to answer the phone this morning. What could they have been talking about? War games?"

"Maybe paint balls?" Was he scoffing at me?

"Paint balls? What do you mean?"

"Balls of paint. It's something people do with air guns. They wear coveralls."

"They have real guns."

"Is that what she said?"

"No, but that's what it sounded like to me."

"Sophie. Listen to the tape again. I'll be over sometime later." He grunted what must have served as a "good-bye." So I did listen to the tape, and it was true. She just said war games. At a house on the beach. And I'd bet my fuzzy pink sleep socks I knew which one it was.

Was Sam right about Deborah? Was she just plain crazy, or maybe crazy as a fox? The biggest burr under my saddle (to borrow a phrase from my husband Monty) was that Deborah alternately referred to our dead neighbor as "Roland" and "Mr. Urquardt." Were they friends or not? They may not have been close friends, but knew each other at least well enough that he had trusted Deborah to take care of his pet bird. Unless she was lying. Maybe she knew about the bird and decided to rescue it. Or sell it. But what about those boxes that the black-jacketed men had delivered to his house? What were they, and what happened to them? Could she have "rescued" those, too?

Speculating about Deborah's character was of no use at this point. Sam would have automatically checked the record for any evidence that she or her boyfriend Hank had been in trouble with the law. I thought that Deborah's war games tip was an enticingly off-the-wall clue and began a search on the Internet. Most of the sites were about video war games, but I found several concerning tournaments involving human beings, and a handful that were sources of equipment, mostly for guns. I studied the pictures and was amazed that these games were allowed. Apparently they were even popular as birthday party activities. Even if boys shot just paint balls the guns looked wicked enough, and these games surely must contribute to society's normalizing aggressiveness and violence.

A website that listed scheduled paint ball tournaments had nothing on the calendar in Florida, though a few were in neighboring states. A link took me to a list of clubs, including one called Tampa Bay Terrors that was changing its name to Tampa Bay Titans. I clicked on the "Contact" email address and wrote: *I'm looking for war games in the Dorado Bay area. Do you know of a war games club that has the Four Horsemen of the Apocalypse as a logo?*

Within ten minutes I had a reply: *Dorado Bay Saracens had crossed swords as their logo. They dropped out of the league. Zoning laws forced them out of their meeting place, a public preserve. Heard they are playing in private tournaments on island.*

I quickly wrote back: *What island is that?*

It was now mid-morning. While I waited for an answer I picked up the phone and punched in Sam's office number and got Jim Purcell instead.

"It's Sophie George. I hope it's not a bother, but I'm calling with a question about zoning laws on behalf of a neighbor."

"Sam's not here, Mrs. George, but I can tell you that we don't do zoning in the police department," he answered in a be-kind-to-old-ladies tone.

"This goes beyond zoning. It's something you might remember, though. Was there an incident" (I implied mayhem and murder) "involving a paint ball game – or worse – that led to out*law*ing" war games in Dorado Bay? And did the games move to an island off the coast?"

"I seem to recall something like that. But it wouldn't have made much of an impression on me at the time."

"No," Sophie said. "Of course not." I thanked him and hung up. The young man was far too sophisticated to worry about neighborhood policing. Within the hour I received a call from Sam.

"What's this about paint ball again? Are you serious?"

"I just wanted to cover the bases, since Deborah mentioned…"

"Forget Deborah, for Pete's sake! You've given me enough trouble with the tie connection. We've just faxed copies of it to 35 police stations up the East Coast. I asked Purcell to scan it into the computer and send a bulletin to every metropolitan station east of the Mississippi River. I'll be the laughing stock."

I wanted to remind him that he had originally told me to forget the tie, that it was a crazy idea, but *he* changed his mind. I didn't, though. This was good. Even though he had many doubts about it, he now seemed to be kind of enjoying the bizarre detail. He was opening up to new ideas. I think my idea of revenge on a global scale, of gang warfare that borrowed from legends and literature and transcended the need to make a quick buck – that provoked his interest. What a way to cap his career, pulling in a bunch of conspirators, madmen, good minds poisoned by politics and revenge.

To be honest, I had almost conceded it could just be that two guys in Dorado Bay bought identical ties at the same store. It happens; you just don't usually notice that if it's stripes or polka dots. But I was not going to interfere now. Let it play out Sam's way, and maybe the result wouldn't be too humiliating to either of us.

Having decided I'd delegate the topic of paint ball, I called my brightest former colleague at the library downtown. Mary Catherine Kneebone recalled the war games incident off the top of her head, and in fifteen minutes got back to me with a citation and said she would FAX the news article. If I wanted the police report, that would take longer.

"Thank you, Mary Kate. This is all I need for now. You are as dependable as ever." The still-employed librarian then launched into ten minutes of complaining about the newly graduated people who called themselves librarians. "We knew books and were not averse to learning about the Wide World Web," she summed up, "but these people" (she always referred to "people" spitting out the word as if she were talking about some substandard species) "are robots. They don't think. They don't read anything off the screen, certainly anything between two covers – unless it's each other's – bodies!" She giggled and no doubt was blushing. I laughed my best lyrical laugh and excused myself on account of "duty calls." I liked leaving a former colleague with the impression that I was a very busy woman these days. I also wished to avoid a conversation that would inevitably mutate into a ruthlessly condemnatory report on the behavior and activities of two gay men who were advancing in the hierarchy of the central branch. Mary Kate was smart in bookish ways, but her conservative, small town upbringing in the Deep South sometimes played havoc with her reasoning powers.

I was eager to continue the search for clues in Roland's family background. I wanted to look at those paintings again, in light of the tie discovery, but the art museum administration was not open on weekends. Only the guards were in the building. Pretty amazing, I thought, that two poorly-paid employees were entrusted with a treasure trove full of expensive art. Unless all the works were of the dubious quality of the Urquardt gift. I mused about the possibility that a museum would arrange to have things stolen periodically to collect the insurance, but I mentally slapped my wrists. I was letting Sam's cynicism rub off on me.

I decided to take advantage of the village fitness center

to spend some quality time exercising my body at the same time I exercised my brain. I might have known there would be no peace there. Several women were using the gym – strange there were no men – and all were eager to talk about the "FOR SALE" sign that had been put up in front of Deborah Conyers's condo.

"I knew it," one said loudly. "She wouldn't hang around after Hank killed himself. Too many memories."

"How do you know he killed himself," I asked innocently.

"News gets around. I heard of the plastic bag trick from the male nurse on night duty at my sister's nursing home. Also heard he was out of money. According to people who knew him, he was a person who couldn't live without money."

"I guess he thought Deborah had some," chimed in another neighbor. Another doubled over her tummy rolls laughing.

"Ha, ha. No money there. She was very, very middle class. Lower. Blue collar. Her dad was a cop."

"Wasn't she married once?" I reminded her.

"Yeah, but to a developer. His big ideas left nothing for her."

"How do you know this?" I asked as calmly as I could. Vultures.

"She told me. She was pretty distraught when Hank died.

Came over looking for a drink every night. My husband finally told me not to let her in or she would empty the liquor cabinet. We aren't rich either, you know."

So I wasn't the only shoulder she cried on, or possessor of a drinks cupboard she exploited.

I drove from the clubhouse to the state park with my folding bicycle, another gift from Robin, in the back seat. I hauled it out and rode along a boulevard leading to the upper middle-class neighborhood that faced the private island. I pedaled in and out of the cul de sacs, seeing no one who wasn't getting into a car. I hoped to spot a public right of way, a place to launch a small boat. No such luck. I rode back to the car, sat there for a few more minutes looking at the city map. I noticed I was close to the area where Deborah's Hank had lived. Tracing the lines with my finger I followed the loop along the shore, remembering that Deborah said it was hard to see from the road, that it hung over the edge, but that it was next to a blue and yellow stucco hacienda with geraniums along the roadside. I loaded up my bike.

It took just five minutes to get there by car. Without slowing down I drove on past the address for a block and turned a corner and parked. I stuck my arm back between the two front seats and grabbed my straw hat, an adjustable walking stick, also from Robin, and his blessed binoculars, off the back seat. In my white pedal pushers and expensively sturdy walking shoes, with a brim to shadow my face and hide my hair, and that high-tech cane, no one would think I was anyone but an elderly resident.

I walked purposefully toward Hank's driveway and continued down the slope to the garage. There was no way around the side, but I could see through the plantings that the house jutted out from the property below the height of the garage, and that the cliff facing the bay was a rather precipitous drop. Backing into a shrub so I could not be seen from anyone on the street, I lifted the binoculars and panned right to left, repeating the slow movement again and again until I thought I had seen as much as I could from that vantage point. Looking cautiously toward the street I danced from shadow to shadow crossing the front lawn, thankful the landscaping was so lush. Small trees had been arranged in a straight line like the Buckingham Palace guard, a formidable barrier between the lawn and the ledge where the very top of the red tile roof could be seen. I could slip through and not be seen from the street.

It took several minutes to go the distance, until I was standing at the wall that divided Hank's property from the neighbor's. There was a clearing there, apparently a couple of trees had died or were removed. I could see past the right side of the house to the water. Some other promontory was in the middle distance. I lifted my binoculars and was surprised to see two very grand houses on it. I thought back to the map of the area. It could be the private island.

Or it could be Concha Key. I started to move down the slope, careful not to trip on a pipe, root, rock, wire, or water sprinkler. It looked like the yard man did very little around this side. It was just dirt and gravel. I found a level spot and ground my heels in to get a good hold on it. I looked over my shoulder to the left where the corner of the roof almost touched the lawn. There was a gap of about five feet. In the gap was a post. On the top of the post was a black canister with a camera lens pointed in my direction. I left the premises quickly.

When I got home the light on my answering machine was blinking. I didn't immediately recognize the number so I ignored it, eager to put the close encounter with an alarm system and the fast drive behind me. I was lucky not to have been stopped for speeding. I would have to tell Sam where I'd been, of course. If my picture had been taken and reported to the security company, he would hear about it. He might be willing to make up some story about sending me there. I was sure he would. Almost positive. Almost. As I changed into fresh clothes I saw the blinking light again and looked at the list of messages. Actually, singular. From the prefix on the number of the only caller, I guessed that it was Emma. I listened:

"Sophie, it's Emma." The voice was bright and cheerful. "I made a phone call to someone on the museum acquisitions committee – can't tell you who – and, yes, they did get paintings from Rudolph Urquardt who lived in that house we were talking about. He wouldn't give them any modern paintings because he was creating a gallery of his own"

I called her back and acknowledged her information confirmed what I had been told. "I went to the museum to see them, Emma. I don't think they ever have been on display. They are grim subjects."

"Oh." She seemed disappointed that I had beaten her to the punch, but then added another tidbit of news. "My friend also is on the donations committee. She said they did approach Roland Urquardt after Rudolph passed on, specifying a need for upkeep on the pieces his brother had donated to their collections. Apparently he laughed at them. He said he couldn't give them money until his father passed on. She said whoever talked to him put 'Try later' by his name. My friend had a copy of the calling list, you see."

"That's what friends are for," I whispered to myself. At the time of the elder brother's death, at least, the father, Otto Urquardt, had been alive.

I called Sam during the commercials between early innings of a Mets baseball game on TV. They were playing at home in Shea Stadium. Sam knew Bobby Valentine.

"I was wondering, have you found Gustav Foucault?" I asked.

Sam explained he had sent word out to New York, and a few other cities. Either they hadn't found him or he didn't come forward. "One woman called in to report her late husband had been a friend and mentor to a young Gustav Foucault. However, she didn't know what happened to him after seminary. She thought he had taken a church somewhere out west.

"Taken a church?" I asked. "He was a clergyman?"

"I suppose so," Sam said, "but it's not enough to go on."

"What denomination was the woman's husband?"

"I'll look at the report a little closer in the morning."

"Okay, enjoy the game," I replied.

SECOND WEEK

Friday, June 19

There were two real puzzles I couldn't leave alone. One was whether or not the old man was still alive, and, of course, why he was living in his divorced wife's family home. The other was Gustav. His life had been in the northeastern United States, but he was still mentioned in an Urquardt obituary. It was if they all remained extended family.

I told Sam what was bothering me and he agreed that, lacking an obit for Otto Urquardt, he still could be alive.

I remembered then that Roland had talked about visiting his grandfather. Perhaps he brought his young stepbrother with him. It would be considered a real treat for a New York child who had probably been cooped up in an apartment in the city or isolated in a country house somewhere. The Foucaults had money and taste, and they probably were wrapped up in one another and their common interest in art. So maybe Otto annually received Gustav with Roland, just as if he were his own stepson. Maybe he and Geneva had remained friends. A divorce between two independently wealthy partners could be amicable.

"That doesn't jibe with what I learned this morning. That minister who befriended Gustav – more like indoctrinated him – was a strict Lutheran. I called his widow and she remembered then that Gustav had chosen Pacific Lutheran Seminary, apparently to get as far from his family as possible."

"I was just wondering if the three brothers were close. He might have spent time in Dorado Bay with his half-brother, at least."

"I don't know about that, but the California connection widens the search to the western U.S."

"Try the Los Angeles area first," I said on a hunch.

"Why would a boy with such a heritage go into the ministry?" I asked Sam.

"You never know what your kids are going to do," Sam said. "Usually it's the opposite of what you want them to do." Which reminded me that I still hadn't heard from Robin. I had better give him a call.

He picked up my call on the first ring. Either he was just dashing out the door or he had caller I.D.

"Mother, it's you. I've been trying to think what to tell you."

"You mean that's why you haven't called me?"

"I mean that I haven't got an address in Egypt yet, but,

yes, I was reluctant to call because I didn't want to hurt your feelings again."

"It hurts when you don't call at all. I didn't even know if you read my letter. It took a long time to write! Meanwhile, my neighbor has been murdered."

Silence. Then, "What?" I smiled to myself. He would be gobsmacked.

"My first case is underway." I explained how I just happened to be the one to discover Roland Urquardt's body.

"Are you sure you didn't plant it there?" he replied, meaning to crack a joke.

"Robin. This is serious."

"I'm sorry. So how far are you and the detective in your detecting?"

"It's so complicated that I can't begin to tell you every detail, but it involves three half-brothers, and probably their father, in criminal activity, perhaps gang warfare." One brother died naturally, the second was Roland, and the third is still out there somewhere, perhaps a minister."

"Doing penance for the family?"

I hadn't thought of that. My son's a genius.

"Have you ever heard of Pacific Lutheran Seminary?" I asked.

"In Berkeley, I believe. It's part of a consortium, with think tanks, research centers, cross-denominational studies, and all kinds of "isms" allowed."

"Is it sort of new? I think he would have been there in the late Sixties or early Seventies."

"It was new then, I'm willing to bet. Look it up."

I then told my son about Deborah Conyers. He had never met her, but he seemed about as convinced of her stories as Sam had been. He also recommended that I take Sam's advice, as long as I was going to be involved. I told him we meet every Friday to plan the next steps and he seemed relieved.

"But Deborah is in California now. She called me from Pasadena, and is going to stay at some other place near L.A."

"Mom, if you are asking me to find her, I just don't have time."

"No, I wouldn't do that to you." Not until I had more information.

Robin told me he was going to Cairo within the month and gave me an office address and phone number for the time being. That would be his headquarters for the duration of the project, which was likely to last three years, but he'd be in Cairo just six months.

After we talked I went to the computer and began to search for information on the seminary. I traced its roots to The Lutheran Church in America that was headquartered in New York City from 1962 before it merged with some other branches of Lutheranism. It had an immigrant heritage, mostly from Germany and Scandinavia, and it flourished on the East Coast as well as the Midwest, and even had congregations in Florida. West Coast, I imagined, with all our Midwesterners. But what did I know?

What was more interesting was that this group was considered the most liberal of the Lutherans in the United States, and that some churches had lost members who had broken off to preserve more pious practices. The LCA was highly centralized and tended to stick to liturgy, in spite of being liberal. But it did begin to have female pastors early on.

I had a quick look at the consortium it belonged to at Berkeley and saw that there were courses in the arts, spirituality, and interdisciplinary studies. The orthodoxy was diverse. Regular church attendance and obeying the priest were not requirements for being a "good Orthodox Christian." And the majority of members who responded to a survey said they wanted to belong to parishes where everyone held the same views. Also, there were a high percentage of second generation clergymen – and presumably women.

"Sophie, where the hell are you?" Sam raged into my ear.

"Omigosh, I forgot it's Friday."

"I waited a half hour after the early bird specials were

gone, and six minutes more worrying that you'd gotten into a wreck."

That was sweet, but I frankly had gotten so off schedule in my head, and he hadn't mentioned it this morning. But of course he was mad at me then, too. And he must be starving, I thought.

"I'll be right there," I said, "I just had something to do on the World Wide Web and everything else flew out of my head." I then added: "I'm eager to see you."

When I arrived at our usual restaurant it was full of noisy people our age and I had a hard time finding him. He was drinking beer and munching on French fried onions, so perhaps he had calmed down.

"We have a lot to talk about," he said, as I laid my purse down in the empty chair and took up the menu.

"Have you ordered?"

"Just this." He took his menu in hand and we were quiet until the cute waitress came and left. I expected a lecture about being at Hank's house, but I was pleasantly surprised. Apparently he didn't know about that yet.

"Sophie, I have to confess," Sam went on, "that up to now I haven't been able to get too worked up about the death of Urquardt who seemed to have no friends or survivors who cared about him enough to claim his remains. The guy might have been into something rotten, but it didn't seem to have much to do with the safety of citizens in Dorado Bay.

"I don't think he was very much involved in anything but family here," I said. "And I am thinking maybe his family wasn't involved in the city either, or we would find more clippings about them. It's not like they were socialites."

"I did spend some time in the archives digging out records of local mafia connections and any gang rivalry. Jim came in to help me, and I took a short break to watch the news. He stumbled upon a feature story from a 1953 *Life* magazine that showed a raid on a 'nightclub in Old Harbor.' That could have been the island. Besides a few embarrassed aldermen, it revealed some locals lights were playing with a Philadelphia gambling syndicate since the 1930s."

"Good for Jim. But were the Urquardts or Foucaults involved?"

"I don't know. The story focused on two brothers in their early-20s who had been shot and killed on the beach near their parents' palatial winter home on Fishhook Key. Their uncle, only slightly older than they were, was found to be running guns to Cuba. That was a surprise to everyone at the time, because he lived an otherwise dull, if solid citizen kind of life as a banker. He was a familiar figure around Old Harbor, walking to work at the brokerage house from his family's Victorian mansion on Front Street."

"That's where Jim's house is," I murmured. He nodded. "In fact, it was the same house. Jim was stunned when he saw the photo."

"But Jim inherited that house from his aunt," I reminded him.

"Yep. And his aunt lived there with her lover. He had done his time and came back to the house he grew up in. She had been waiting for him. Of course her parents wouldn't let her marry a convict. They had to live 'in sin.'"

"Did Jim know this?"

"He did know his aunt 'lived in sin.'" In fact he was the only member of the family who ever spoke to her again."

"No wonder she left the house to him, another black sheep."

"Jim admitted he is not in touch with his family either."

"I have some news, too," I said. I summarized Ella's report on Rudolph and Roland's connections to the museum. I explained that I had seen the paintings and what they seemed to be about: war, rape, and ravaging town and countryside.

"The Apocalypse?"

"Maybe we're getting closer."

"It's only circumstantial."

"They also were by Gustav Foucault, the father. He wasn't very good." I then told him about the Lutheran seminary Gustav the son, had trained at. "I think it's possible that he, too, had differences with his family."

"But his family was his mother and father."

"And Roland, who was living with his mother after the divorce. At first I thought they would be friends. But maybe there was a problem between them. He never mentioned that he had a brother to either me or Deborah."

"He never mentioned much of anything."

"True."

"There's something else. Otto Urquardt was alive when his ex-wife and her husband died in a plane crash." Sam was silent. I continued, "I checked and have not been able to come up with a death notice for him."

"He might have died anywhere. It isn't clear that he even was living here. He might have been traveling a lot when his ex-wife remarried. It was her house."

"Why wouldn't they report his death in Dorado Bay?

"Well, as you pointed out, he wasn't much of a citizen."

"How about we go to the island and see that house up close?" I asked.

"We?"

"You and I," I said. "We can sneak up on it and no fuss, no muss, just some fishing gear and my binoculars."

"No way, Jose," he replied.

"How about going for a swim?'

He harrumphed and said 'Talk to you tomorrow, if you're still among the living."

Saturday, June 20

I was just coming in the door after my walk in a really good mood when the phone started to ring. It was Sam. He had found out about my visit to Hank's house.

"So! You forgot to mention your little reccy. Are you joining Purcell in the ranks of architecture historians? What the hell did you expect to find?"

"They turned me in?"

"They? Nobody's at that house. Those cameras belong to us."

"But why? Are you done with Deborah or not?"

"It's not about Deborah. It's about her boyfriend."

"You're investigating Hank? And you didn't tell me?"

"Couldn't. It's CIA. And we're not investigating Hank. He was an agent."

"What?" Sam sounded very pompous all of a sudden. I could see him all puffed up, chest out, bouncing on his toes, imagining my surprised expression.

"He was watching the Urquardt Foucault island."

"Why?"

"That's the rub. We're not sure. He was supposed to be taking pictures and keeping journals – nothing on a computer – but they haven't been found. He could get close to the island in his own boat and no one would think it strange because he lived just across the way."

"Do you think Deborah knew this?"

"I doubt it, but you'll have to ask her – if she calls again. If she doesn't call, then she probably knows and she's scared as shi-heck."

"So can we go see what's going on there this afternoon?"

""I have other plans, sweetie," Sam said, ambiguously. "Maybe tomorrow."

Deborah did call again. Before she could even say a word, I tore into her: "Deborah, you house is for sale! You didn't tell me you weren't coming back!"

"I don't own the house, Sophie. I paid until the end of this month. I guess they assumed I was moving out."

"They can't do that? Who's your landlord?"

"Roland was."

"Roland? Roland Urquardt? Our neighbor?"

"Yes. But the check didn't go right to him. He has a property manager."

"Had."

"Yes. But it's all right. I am staying here for a while. We're in Pasadena and tomorrow we are going to White Angel Ranch. It's a kind of spiritual community. There's a very nice man who heads the whole thing. His name is

Gustav. He knows what happened to Hank. He has offered me a place to rest for a while, a pretty little cottage, until I can get myself together. He said he'd find me a job."

"This is crazy. Hank was with the CIA. What does a spiritual community leader know about the criminal world?" I said it before I realized it. I meant to get to this topic more gently, in case she didn't know. "I'm sorry," I began to apologize.

"It's all right, Sophie. He told me."

"Hank?"

"No. My, er, host. He was working with them. That's all I know. The club, the car, the house, they were all part of the undercover work."

"And the suicide?"

"It wasn't suicide. Someone found out. I feel much better now. That's all I know now. Gotta go."

Feel better? Hank was murdered? These thoughts were dazzling. But I shouted, "Wait! Where are you right now?"

"In a pretty B&B. You wouldn't believe this, but the Rose Bowl Parade comes right up this street, and it looks like a really ritzy neighborhood. It's lined with those extremely tall, skinny palm trees. I don't know how they stand up."

"Does the B&B have a name?"

"Rose something, of course. Gotta go. Someone else needs this phone." That was it. She certainly sounded happier, but I wondered now how she felt about Hank. Was she part of his cover, too? Did he use her? Did she care? Or was this new man in her life – her newest savior – stepping into Hank's shoes?

Then I smiled broadly to myself. I was right. Deborah *was* involved in the Urquardt case. I could hardly wait to talk to Sam.

"I'd say he's not stepping into Hank's shoes; she's stepping out of her panties," Sam said in his especially crude manner. He'd had a couple of drinks, and I soon found out where.

"It was just a gut feeling," Sam said in recalling how he decided to head for the Minotaur on Ambassador Key. It was a club and casino that attracted a certain stratum of Dorado Bay society, trust fund babies without the edge for their fathers' killer sports but still needy of risk and achievement. At four p.m., members and their guests were just beginning to pull up their yachts and freshen up in the private "cabanas" in the condo towers. The men slipped onto barstools in a colonnaded room with a frieze depicting marauders, half-men, half-beast, carrying off nubile, half-naked women. The games opened at a civilized six p.m. Parties of ten or twelve assembled around the high stakes tables in their starched tuxes and sequined gowns. The drinking and gambling went on until two a.m., but the crowds tapered off when the fondling started around eleven, leaving the most desperate rollers to duke it out on the baize.

"The last female had gone before I came out of the dark corner where I had watched the regulars on the centuries-old journey to ruin. I walked over to the croupier, and mumbled into his ear: Anything unusual here? He gave me a stony-faced glance, and then jerked his chin up sideways. I took that as a sign to pay attention to Jonas Peabody, the great-great-grandson of an old Floridian who made his fortune in railroad coaches in the 1880s. His small piece of the fortune dwindling, Jonas has all but set up housekeeping at the club. The word is out he lives in one of the dozen or so nouveau mansions on the main drive into the club. It isn't his, but belongs to a woman in her mid-thirties whose money is a little newer and likely to last his lifetime at least. She was sitting at the casual bar around the corner, rubbing elbows and thighs with a golden boy her age wearing gold chains nestled in curly dark chest hair."

Sam went on to describe the atmosphere. He had kept his eyes on Jonas, whose eyes were puffy and darting around the table perhaps trying to sum things up and understand where he was heading tonight. Everybody else seemed tense, making sure to keep track of their cards. They all knew Jonas was a poor loser and likely to knock the cards out of formation when his luck played out. More than once this had led to accusations of cheating followed by a bloody brawl.

A clap on his shoulder unfocused Sam, and as he wheeled around he was enveloped in the stench of sweet cigar. Marcus Torchier, his nemesis for decades.

"He asked me, 'You still around, old chap? I thought you had been made redundant and high-tailed it to the mountains where your ancestors built their empire.' He was referring to the Scots-Irish hillbillies in North Georgia who gave my mother to my dad, a New York Jew down south on a lark with a bunch of railroad worker friends. The two of them struggled to build up a small tourist camp into a resort that took off in the 1960s. I tried to look unfazed. This guy is one of about a half dozen local crime lords whose scores I have been unable to even over all my years as a detective."

Sam said nobody could ever pin Torchier down. He was brazen, hanging around the casinos and heading development of old shipping yards into substandard apartments that were rented to illegal aliens, fifteen people in two rooms. The Brit's name actually was Torchier, as he was by paternity French. He had attended an Oxford college, owing to a snooty mother and a *grandpere* who was English and in the Cabinet "bet-ween the wahhhs." In Dorado Bay he had a fleet of restaurants, from top flight to the mock pub in the back of a boat anchored at the casino. The pub and boat had been brought over from the London Docklands when it became a renewal district a few years ago. Marcus Torchier had money in the Canary Wharf scheme, and spent some small part of it salvaging London history and spreading it around the world. He said he got the idea from the sale of the London Bridge to Arizonans.

"I was careful. I said jovially, 'They kept me on, Torch.' I told him I was glad to see he was still alive. Then I got careless. I asked, 'Isn't this your night to rub up drunk old dames?' I referred to scene a few years ago when a well-known socialite, age around 70, and typically intoxicated by five o'clock, had roared with laughter when the phony rogue, who wore a walrus moustache then, tried to nuzzle her. Apparently she screamed, 'Don't Torcher me!' It became a byword in that crowd for any unwanted affection."

"So how did he react?"

"To her, or to me?"

"To you!"

"He took offense and grabbed me by the arm. He snarled, 'You try to humiliate me, old fellow, and I'll have you kicked to Timbuktu.' His two IRA-type companions stepped forward. I nodded at each and kept my mouth shut. If I had been ten years younger, I night have tried to take them on."

"I'm glad you didn't," I said, suspecting that the threat didn't matter at all, but the "old fellow" part did.

"So that's when I went home in a funk and fell asleep in front of the TV."

I was quite touched by his humble confession, if you want to know. This was the first time he really let me inside his head, and I at last felt we really had become friends. But he was so humble that, after we hung up, I started to wonder if he'd made the whole thing up, and was really out with some other woman, maybe even at the casino. A little detail he didn't include. Oh, so what? I just wish he were as forthcoming about the details of our work together.

And then he was. About half an hour later, just as I was nodding off over my bedtime reading, the phone rang again.

"I have good news," he said. Fully awake after our talk, he'd made for the coffee pot and then the computer. An e-mail sent at about 9 p.m. reported that the NYPD gofer got two more matches for the ties.

"Damned if the little librarian wasn't right after all," he said teasingly. He had received pictures as attachments. That made four dead men, two in New York and two in Dorado Bay wearing the same tie as Urquardt. None of the murders had been solved.

He described the two New York cases: One of the men had only recently come to the U.S. from Venezuela. He had a German name. He was found dead in an alley alongside a small apartment building where he had rented a studio apartment six months earlier. Shot in the back, up close. There were no relatives to claim his body and no apparent friends. He had taken a job in the laundry of the French Hospital about two miles from where he was living. He was a good worker, but quiet. A co-worker identified him but could tell the police nothing about the man except that he rode a bicycle to work. He never fraternized with the others working in his department, though he had been invited out to have drinks. Some thought he might have had a second job.

The other murder had taken place in the men's restroom of a Greek restaurant a couple of blocks from Central Park. There was loud music on the Saturday night it happened, some sort of festival taking place, so no one heard shots. The bullets went into the victim's back. An inebriated diner had come through a wooden swinging door opening onto a row of urinals and stumbled over the crumpled body. They had been in the same large party. It became a chaotic situation; most of the diners managed to leave before the police came. Most had slapped more than enough cash down on the table, so it was a good night for the restaurateur. The witness – that is, the diner who found the body, claimed he was not a regular in this group, that he had met some of them at a private party that he had been invited to by another friend. That other friend claimed he did not know who the dead man was and he could not say who might have been in the group. "Obfuscation," Sam concluded.

"What do you think? Were they related incidents?"

"Don't know. This thing is still unfolding."

"That reminds me, I forgot to tell you what I found out," I said.

"What you got?"

"Well, it's about the island. I found out there used to be a paint ball war games team in Dorado Bay – the Saracens – that got into trouble."

"Yeah. I remember. Someone's dog got hit. Busted his rib cage. They had to put him down. The neighbors around the park where they played made a ruckus. The team had to quit."

"They left the league but didn't disband. I found out from a reliable source that they now play on 'a private island.'"

"What makes you think it's our island?" Sam seemed impatient. Sophie bit her tongue.

"I'm ninety-nine-and-nine-tenths sure," I said, mimicking him. "They might have been practicing for the real thing: War games. War crimes. Military law. Retribution."

"You mean you think the Apocalypse murder victims were sought out for things they did in the war? This is nuts! Roland Urquardt never served in any war."

"But maybe he was involved in the retribution part, working with his brother and father. These other victims – do you know if they had military experience? Specifically, were they in charge of any military operations? I'm thinking Europe."

"Whoa! This is a pretty wild hare, Sophie. It would make a lot more sense if they were connected to the New York or Philadelphia mafias. This is Florida."

"You don't think there are enough retired military types here?"

"I think there are plenty – but vengeance?"

"A lot of people lost family members in the wars in Europe."

"So let me get this straight: You are thinking the firm the murder victim did work for had a vigilante division?"

"Something like that." I looked toward the window and the pond, where there no longer were any signs of what happened to Roland Urquardt. This put me in my lecturing mode:

"Paint ball games are considered harmless. But do you know what the outcome is? Not physical destruction, most of the time, but moral destruction. The video games are the most insidious purveyors of aggressive behavior. They are extensions of boardroom politics – or, I should say, boardroom politics come out of the violent, competitions we enjoy as 'games.' War games are teaching devices. Some would say they are hardening us to the real world and the need to survive. I say they are changing us – changing us, Sam – just like TV has changed the brain activity of children – these war games, whether they are on machines in malls, on the Internet, or shooting paint balls at other men, have fueled our resolve to 'beat' the others. *Beat!* Doesn't that speak of our violent natures? We're always beating someone. And since they are just games we think of beating someone not only as normal but as recreation."

My eyes were moist, my torso stiff inside my nightgown. As I paused to consider what more I could say to convince him, he spoke gently.

"Sophie, you sound fighting mad. Don't be so violent." I had to laugh.

We hung up and a moment later the phone rang again and I hesitated but finally picked up the receiver.

"It's me again," said Deborah with a breathy voice. "I have only a minute. Here's where I am." She named a ranch and a road and said it was northeast of Pasadena. Then she hung up. The message had taken all of 15 seconds. I called Sam's number.

"I had another call from Deborah. I think she needs our help. I'm going there."

"Where?"

"White Angel Ranch northeast of Pasadena. Sam, something's gone wrong. She's laying a trail for us."

"*We'll* check on it," he reassured me.

"*I* want to go. She'll be frightened. She'll talk to me."

"I don't think so, Sophie. We don't know yet. Don't let your imagination carry you away."

"I think her trouble has something to do with the island warriors," I added firmly, holding my desire to spit out the facts like nails – violently. I reminded him of the location of Hank's house right across from that island, with about a half mile of shallow water between them. If Sam was thinking Roland Urquardt's father and maybe even his grandfather had commanded a ring of hoodlums or even just wannabe hoodlums, the hoodlums' heirs might still be active. "Their purposes were vague back in the Forties, but their purposes may have changed," I said. I thought to myself that the neckties either have to be better understood or ruled out of the equation, and we had to know who Deborah's protector, "the spiritual leader," was – now. Could it be Gustav Foucault, the white sheep in the black flock? I was ready to find out. But I'd have to take it a step at a time.

"Well," I responded. "Deborah believes that she is in a safe environment. It's a religious community. But the leader told her Hank was with the CIA. How do you think he knew that? And, by the way, Deborah let it slip that the house she lived in here was owned by Roland Urquardt aka Shady Lane Properties.

Surprisingly, Sam seemed much more interested in the rental than in Deborah's current situation. "I wonder how she came to rent that one?" he wondered aloud. "Can you find out if Deborah was dating Hank when she moved into that house, or if she was there before she met him?"

I said I'd try. I knew what Sam was thinking. If Hank found the rental for Deborah, he probably knew Urquardt owned it, and he then could connect with him more naturally. But as far as I understood it, Hank didn't spend any time at Deborah's house; she was always at his, or at the yacht club. So if Deborah lived there before meeting Hank, then it could mean Hank started dating her because of her location. That would break her heart. But, no, the house wouldn't matter if there was no real communication between Roland and Hank. This looked like a brick wall, a coincidence. Still, I felt it would help to know when Roland bought the property. I couldn't look at real estate records until Monday.

Sam had switched the topic to the houses on the island.

"I don't know why it's been so hard to find out who actually lives in this place, places, I should say. It looks like a family compound. The newer ones could be second generation."

"The problem is," I explained, "there are no addresses, *per se*. It's all one property – the island. Belongs to a trust, remember? West Coast Holdings. Not much of a clue to anyone's identity.

"I'll put Purcell on it," Sam offered.

"I talked to Jim this morning," I mentioned. "He didn't seem too happy. I was going to ask him to have lunch with me, but he declined rather brusquely. Are you working him too hard?" I knew the reason was that he didn't want another research assignment.

"His social life is taking a hit." The younger policeman had come a long way in a short time, from speed patrol to junior detective in two short years, Sam explained. "The main reason I asked for him to be my assistant is that 'pussy

Purcell' was the butt of jokes in every other division, and came pretty close to being left in mortal danger more than once. "Homophobes," Sam pronounced. "The academy's full of them."

"I hope he's grateful to you."

"He's doing a good job. Purcell has talents."

"He probably wants your job when you retire."

"He did say he'd like someday to have a job like mine where no one could question his judgment."

"You mean no one ever questions your judgment, Sam?" I asked, mock-astonished.

"Not more than once."

I thought that was pretty witty comeback, but since I wanted to make a point, I suggested we give Purcell a break from the lonely job of research and invite him to go to the island with us.

Sunday, June 21

I was doing my stretching exercises in bed, lifting one leg and pointing my numb toes at the ceiling, then the other. I was just beginning to feel the blood flow when the phone rang. Rolling to my left side I could just reach the receiver with my right hand.

"Just checking to see if you were up. What time do you

want to go?

"I'm ready anytime," I said. "I'll bring my bike. Do you have one?"

"I could borrow one from Jim. He has three or four."

"How long has it been since you've ridden a two-wheeler, Sam?"

He slammed the receiver down. I called him right back and apologized, using the excuse that I hadn't had my coffee. We agreed to meet at the state park main parking lot at ten. The park would be busy on a Sunday with hikers, and no one would pay any attention to us. We'd each bring a fishing pole to look less suspicious if we had to rent a boat.

As I drove out the south gate to Bridgewater, though, I turned around and circled through my neighborhood. It was quite interesting that all the nearby FOR SALE signs were Shady Lane Properties. Were they all owned by Roland Urquardt? I'd be interested to know what the prices were. Maybe he was keeping them empty on purpose.

Sam was waiting at a picnic table and he had a cheerful and relaxed Jim with him. I had brought enough coffee and rolls so we looked like we were just pausing during a walk in the preserves like so many other Sunday morning nature worshippers.

They had things to tell me. Sam had asked Purcell to organize a "tie watch" among the police all over the Dorado Bay area. Within two hours he was rewarded with the news that three such ties had recently been noted by the long-time clerk at a convenience store near the southern bridge to the keys, just a few miles from the island retreat. As soon as we finished our coffees we would check in at that store a few blocks from the park.

"I'm dumbfounded," Sam admitted as they drove to the Go-Pak.

"Right under our noses," I added.

Sam recognized the burly Italian who used to have his own grocery on the highway going north of town, before the Interstate put him out of business. He was nervously eager to talk, probably unsure of how close he came to being robbed.

"You notice these things behind a counter. I thought it was a coincidence when the second guy came in. You know, a gag tie stocked by a local store, something new, a shocker, attention-getter. I asked the third customer – just a couple days ago – where he had bought it, but he just stared me down. You'd a thought I had asked where he buys his Trojans." He glanced at Sophie and added, "Sorry, ma'am."

Luigi had watched that last man's car leave the parking lot and turn onto the bridge to the keys.

We drove to a neighborhood police station to borrow sturdy lightweight bikes for Jim and Sam. There on the wall was a highly detailed map of the coastal area this station patrolled. It resembled the one at the hardware store.

"Look at this," Purcell whispered. We all crowded together as he traced a narrow strip of land that extended from the east end of the marina to the little island we intended to explore. The officer said he didn't think it was used for anything but fishing.

"We won't need a boat," Sam said. He asked a policeman holding down the fort if they could borrow three windbreakers with hoods, suggesting this would make us less noticeable in the quarter-mile open space. He explained what we were going to do.

"My guess is that it was built there in recent years to prevent boats from speeding close to the mainland shore," suggested a sandy-haired sergeant who knew Sam from training under him decades earlier. He clearly wanted to impress his one-time mentor. "See those lots?" He pointed on the map at an avenue running close to the shore. "There are some ranch-style houses here that were built in the 1960s. They don't look like much from the road, but, location-location-location, they are now worth millions."

We left Sam's car in the station parking lot, then headed our bikes toward the marina. Just as we were approaching it, Sam, who was leading the pack, gestured left to a sandy track heading toward the water, posted with a 15 mph sign. We soon were enveloped in dark green branches and quiet. We parked a hundred yards down and took out our fishing poles. Sam again took the lead. We began to hear the waves whishing onto the sand. At the end of the road was a launching dock and to its right was the narrow causeway that stretched from the mainland to the private island. It was sandy soil shot through with roots of some low shrub. Jim took the lead now. He walked his bike up to the top and after testing it for a few hundred yards came back and motioned for us to follow. Sam told us to pull up the hoods on our parkas. The sandy path between the shrubs was not wide enough to bicycle without getting the fishing poles, balanced on our handlebars, tangled in branches. We followed Jim's example and lay our poles under the shrubs, one on top of the other. He covered them with more branches.

The weeds in the path made it hard to ride in line. Miraculously, there were no incidents, no stopping, no signs of anyone using this isolated part of the bay for fishing today.

Once we had reached the other side, where there was protection inside the mangrove woods, we stopped to use my binoculars to estimate our distance from any other human activity on the island. We could see we were closer to the old crenellated house than the newer ones. Rather than head up the paved road which most likely was the same one I had seen from the park on that first reccy, we buried our bikes in the overgrowth and set out on foot, following a dry streambed.

"What's a stream like this doing on an island?" I asked.

"Methinks it's manmade," Sam responded, but offered no further speculation.

Soon we had a clear view of the house made of gray stones. The back walls were, however, simply concrete, as bleak as a 1920s city hall.

"Here," Jim said as he motioned toward a fallen tree trunk with a limb attached that offered a perch about eight feet off the ground. There were enough bends in the good-sized branches to form backrests, and the foliage, still relatively fresh, curled around our shoulders.

"Front row seats," I whispered as big, black cars began to congregate on the flat lawn at this back side of the house. Six garage doors faced our direction, and four were wide open. The front hoods of more black limousines could be seen gleaming in the dark interior.

"Mercedes, Lincoln, Mazda, Lexus," Sam was chanting. "All the same beguiling color."

"Looks like a funeral," Jim quipped, but then pressed his lips tightly. I guess he realized grim humor was not appropriate to the occasion. One of the sheltered cars glided out of its bay and took the paved road heading our way. As it passed close to the blind, I watched through binoculars then handed them to Sam who nodded. A uniformed chauffeur drove a single passenger, huddled in the back seat. When they had passed us by, we quietly let ourselves down from the camouflage and moved closer to the road, intending to follow. The Florida license plate was undistinguished. Sam wrote it down.

"Doggone. No bumper stickers," I joked. Surprisingly, the driver was going so slowly that we had to stay a little behind and in the ditch. Then, unexpectedly, the car accelerated and lunged off the paved road onto a gravel track, heading back toward the Gulf rather than toward the mainland.

"My fault," Sam commented. "Let's go back and get the bikes. I hope he didn't spot us."

"I'll mark their turnoff with this scarf in my pocket," I offered, tying the red and blue plaid square around a branch but close to the trunk. No one would notice it who wasn't looking for it.

By the time we walked to where we had left the bikes and returned to the marked road, fifteen minutes had lapsed. The gravel road looked fresh, and led eventually to a locked cattle gate which we climbed easily, with the youngest of us offering to lift the bikes over the bars. At this point we heard shooting. Pop. Pop. Backing into bushes Sam used the binoculars to locate the source of the noises and showed Jim and me a third house, this one smaller and informal, a Tudor cottage of sorts. A limousine, probably the limousine we had followed, was parked in front. We couldn't see the license plate because the uniformed driver was leaning casually against it, his arms folded. The door of the house opened and another man, wearing a *black leather jacket*, strode down two huge flagstone steps and shook hands with the chauffeur who had opened the trunk and lifted out a wheelchair. They both moved to the passenger side and the two lifted a hunched figure to a more-or-less upright position between them, supporting him as he walked a couple steps, until he could sink into the seat.

The old man seemed to be shaking his head in negative fashion, and the leather-jacketed aide turned the wheelchair around and took him up some flagstones set in a sequence of small terraces, and then into the house. In a few minutes, as we watched the windows, they came out on a second floor balcony. If they had looked down into the woods they might have seen us, but they were gazing off in the middle distance. Pop. Pop-pop-pop. We three automatically looked back over our shoulders. Sam immediately climbed up a tree

"Be careful, Sam," I cautioned, noting that its branches were leafless, a mess of sharp twigs. He carefully made his way down again.

"Let's go, he said. "I saw a small structure we can climb and get a better view." Crouching, we made our way to a metal shed about half the size of an 18-wheeler. A ladder was permanently fastened to one end. The building had a slightly pitched, metal roof. Sam climbed up first and demonstrated a safe position, arranging himself on his stomach, head slanted upward, and Jim and I copied him.

He handed the binoculars to Jim and took his bulky police issue radiophone out of his pocket; quietly, he spoke some numbers. While he waited for an answer, he scribbled some notes in the little book he always carries in a pocket. I was braced on my forearms, looking over the peak of the roof at the panorama, and then felt a hand push me down as a loud pop sounded close by. I tucked my head down, laying my cheek on the sun-warmed metal. Right below us, in the shadow of the shed, I could see the top half of a man sitting on a horse. He wore the regimental black leather. I could smell the blended aromas of horse and paint. "My Old Horse Paint" came into the foreground of my extensive repertoire of silly songs. The horse softly whickered and tossed his head. It just stood there in one place. The rider seemed to be watching something intently. Sam nudged me and whispered to slide upward on the slant of the roof, keeping my hood over my hair. Then we could see another man staggering out from the wooded area into sunlight. He was wearing shorts and no shirt, sneakers not boots, and a narrow black blindfold. He came forward until he disappeared from our view, brushing the surface of the shed, apparently unaware of the horseman's presence around the corner, about ten feet away. I could hear his panting and what sounded like a whimper of a pup.

Another shot rang out and I heard a thump. The man appeared again, this time rolling on the ground toward the horse's legs.

"There are bullets in those guns," I rasped to Sam.

"Pellets," Sam said. "Remember, it's a game. He's playing dead."

But then more shots ratcheted low to the ground leaving holes in the man's bare back. The horseman dismounted and bent over the crumpled body, then dragged it off to the side. I cringed and glanced at Sam. He was staying flat, sucking in his gut, his hands cupped around the back of his head, sliding back down the sloping tin roof feet first. I followed, pushing myself backward as quietly as I could, playing back the scene in my head, hardly believing what I had seen.

The victim had not been running. He had been staggering, unable to see where he was. This was no contest. I looked again. The "body" lay there face down with blood beginning to pool in the dirt. Two additional "soldiers" came to the scene and pulled the body about 20 yards beyond the shed. The body was now hidden behind shrubs, but we watched as they took a body bag out of the back of a van and a few moments later hoisted it awkwardly into a limousine that had silently driven to the spot. All this time the war game was still going on, racket-tatting and zooz-ing amongst the more distant trees.

"Is he really just stunned?" I whispered in Sam's ear. I raised my head to look toward the balcony where the man in the wheelchair also had binoculars. "Sam, let's go. They might be able to see us," I said urgently, tugging at his elbow. He also glanced toward the house and nodded, then showed me where to wiggle sideways and backward off the edge of the roof, dropping to the corner away from the action.

"Where's Jim?" I asked when I realized he wasn't with us.

"C'mon."

We scrambled through the ditch to our bikes in the bushes and saw that Jim's was gone. Had he run off scared? On his first dangerous stake-out? I hoped not.

"Where's Jim?" I asked again.

"I'm sure he's all right."

We quickly wheeled across the narrow causeway, then detoured into the confusion of shady streets and alleys in the waterfront neighborhood, eventually circling around and turning back to the neighborhood station where we had started out. There Sam put the crime-busting machine in motion using the hotline to headquarters, confirming his earlier location. He then turned to his former trainee. He simply repeated that we'd heard rifle shots on the island and perhaps he'd want to check on it. The sergeant got up and put on his holster and jacket. We left the building together, but headed to separate cars.

"What will he do?" I asked Sam.

"Maybe nothing," Sam replied.

"Why would he not do anything?" I asked.

"He may be paid off. We'll know in a few hours."

I couldn't see it helping either way. If a patrol was sent out to call on the island homeowners they were likely to get blank stares and denials of having heard the alleged gunshots. More than likely, the members of the war games organization would be long gone. But what about the old man? Would he be back in his big house, and would he be alone? Would a servant be living there, instructed to keep him out of sight? Was this old man Otto Urquardt? Was he in charge of the whole operation?

Forty-five minutes later the two of us, exhausted, were nonetheless congratulating each other for riding bikes without falling. In between swigs of bourbon, Sam reviewed what we had seen and speculated about its meaning. "I suppose the old man could be Otto Urquardt, if he's still alive."

"I'll look deeper for his obituary tomorrow."

"I'll look back at the police archives tonight," Sam said aggressively.

"Did Jim run away?" I finally had the nerve to ask.

"Nope," Sam answered, but said no more. I broiled some hamburgers and Sam tossed a salad and we hardly talked, but listened to Beethoven's Ninth to soothe our souls. Toward the end he had his eyes closed, and I was afraid I'd have to wake him up, but they snapped open as soon as the music ended abruptly.

It was after eleven, an hour past my usual bedtime, but I was wide awake, exhausted but stimulated, seeing the shape of the thing looming up before us. It seemed to be a kind of cult. I imagined there might even be exactly 666 members. If Sam was right, they started out in New York and worked up and down the East Coast as required. Exactly who or what they protected we still had to imagine. Maybe a little bit of everything. It might be an organization of hit men. More knowledge of Roland Urquardt's comings and goings was badly needed.

The phone rang. It was Sam, who said he wanted me to know he appreciated my persistence. I was pleased but still worried about getting Deborah back.

"Have you heard from Jim?" I asked.

"That's why I'm calling. You won't believe what he did. I should reprimand him, but I think he was justified, going off on his own."

"Where?" I demanded.

"He went to check out the old house. Don't say anything more. We'll both be over in the morning."

Monday, June 22

My Florida room was becoming quite the hub of the investigation. Well, of course it all started here. Even I sometimes forget that. When Jim arrived with Sam the two were in animated conversation.

"Detective Sergeant Purcell has a confession to make," Sam said as soon as he was stirring *faux* sugar into his coffee. "Go ahead," he motioned to the young man, whose eyes were crinkling at the corners. I had never seen him do that before.

"When I left you sliding off the roof after the 'paint ball' tournament, I saw the old man in the wheelchair disappear back inside. I decided to follow the car if it drove back to the mansion. I had some vague idea of getting inside and looking around. I learned a lot more about the layout after we talked the other night, Sophie; I looked at the university library where I found plans in Special Collections under Local Architecture."

"What made it such a sensation when it was built?" I asked.

"Everybody else was building in the Spanish Mission style. This was Italian, by way of England. It's supposed to be a copy of the Queen's House in Greenwich. The designer was Inigo Jones, who introduced Palladian style to London."

"Spare her the details," Sam interrupted.

"This is interesting," I fought back. "It tells us something about the family."

"Well, they weren't English," Jim replied. "They were just *nouveau riche*."

What's the inside like?"

"I had the floor plan from Summerson's *Architecture in Britain, 1530-1830*" he went on. When I got to the house I didn't see any activity, even though the old man's driver had pulled up to the front of it. But it seemed like nothing else was going on. I supposed the players had left."

"Did you go in?" I was eager to know.

"Not at first. There was something really foreboding about the silence, and I don't mind saying that I was cautious without backup."

"You could have asked," Sam interjected.

"I know. But I hadn't really been convinced it was necessary to go in. I just wanted to know where the old man went."

"But you didn't se him actually lifted out of the car?"

"I was too late."

"So you had to go in."

"I decided to examine the exterior first. It was a pretty ugly house, in spite of its pedigree. It's gray all over. And it was absolutely silent in the grounds except for waves on the beach and birds making noises. "

"No guards?"

"One of the first things I worried about. I traced the balustrade around the rooftop. Nothing, nobody, was there. Then I checked every window within view for signs of life. There was no evidence of inhabitants in the rooms on my side. I moved around the perimeter. It was getting on toward dusk by then. At the front, the bottom floor was mostly underground, so the structure looked more like a municipal building than a residence. There was only one major entrance a couple of steps down from the ground level, between curving staircases leading upward on either side. These ended on a terrace. There was no doorway into the house from the terrace as far as I could tell, only French windows shut tight all across the front. It was still light enough for the rooms not to be lit."

"I would be afraid someone might be looking out toward the lawn," I said. "Normal people would."

"What's normal?" Sam asked. He gave me a sour look. Jim continued his narration.

"The floor plan showed that the house was really two rectangular structures, one in front and one in back, connected by porticos. They had no walls, just columns. I could see right through them, so I knew if anyone was around, they could see me if I walked there. If the layout of the rooms was like the English original, I needed to get to the top story where the private suites would be. If I couldn't find an open window on the ground level, I would have to climb up on something."

"The roof of a portico," Sam clarified.

"I got lucky. I circled close to the foundation inside the courtyard, heading toward the back section, and at the corner of that a sash window was pushed up halfway for someone to make a quick perambulation of the garden, if 18th century novels are to be believed. I climbed in and found myself in a small room that was furnished like a sitting room, with enormous gilt-framed mirrors on two walls to make it seem larger. Frankly, it seemed like a time capsule. This is when I decided I had better call Sam."

"I came right to the gated entrance in a squad car, and it was a good thing my bike was in the trunk because the gate was locked."

"Why didn't you call me?" I complained.

"Sophie, don't whine," Sam said. "I couldn't be responsible for a citizen in this situation, but I am responsible for a member of the force!"

"Of course."

"Anyway," Jim continued, "it was good to have him there. Sam reminded me of things I didn't remember from training, like staying away from mirrors so no one could see our reflections if they happened to glance through the open door."

"Were all the rooms furnished with 17th century antiques?" I asked. Sam rolled his eyes. I was thinking it might help identify who was living there. The next generation always changes things.

"It was too dark to see the wood, but I bumped into a settee and ran my hand over the taffeta-like, iridescent fabric," Jim said with authority. "I hadn't seen material like this outside a museum. I also looked up and saw the Adams-style, decorated plaster ceiling."

"This was the real thing," I said.

"Yes. I think it was probably very well done."

"We couldn't saw a hole in the ceiling," Sam muttered.

"We reached a door that probably led to a private bedchamber. Sam put his ear to the oak panel, then shook his head. We opened it. Instead of another room there was a hallway, with a crossroads to the left. On the short hallway we were in there was a narrow staircase. The larger hallway ahead we figured was the one dividing the wing. There were six doors on each side, all the same. We decided the old man's room would be in a special suite, probably at the front, where the car had been parked."

"At the end of the corridor was an exit to the other portico rooftop, our bridge. I looked at the plan again and saw what I thought was a reception room. We went out on the portico roof and crept along until we came to the front section. We had to break a window this time. Again, there was a corner room with a door to the small and large hallways. This time there was a double door on the right, next to where the top of a staircase should be, according to the English manor plan. Servants could easily use this route coming from downstairs to the master's room. "

"What makes you think that old man was still the master?" I asked. I thought they had been making a huge assumption.

"Perhaps 'master' isn't the right word," Jim said. "But this was a grand suite of rooms. And we saw things there…" He looked at Sam with a question in his expression.

"Tell her," Sam said.

"The bedroom was in a state of disarray, to put it politely."

"Pee-yew," Sam added, pinching his nose. "Worse than a nursing home."

"We had to use our emergency environmental hazard masks, those paper ones we carry," Jim said, demonstrating by covering his nose and mouth. "It was a combination of stale air, dirty food plates, a filthy bathroom, and the odor of sick and dying human flesh."

"You found a body?"

"Not yet," Sam cautioned.

'The bedclothes were twisted off the bed and lay grotesquely across the immense Chinese carpet, like someone had been dragged out onto the floor. No blood, however."

"That's very literary," I commented. "You should be a writer."

"Get on with it, Purcell. We should be in the office by now." Sam interjected. But Purcell nodded thanks at me before he continued.

"We checked the bathroom – a mess as well – and moved toward the next room of the suite, which overlooked the garden. There was nothing there but a writing desk, a couple of armchairs, and absolute silence. A door across that room led to what the English call a 'box room.' We were in complete darkness now, bumping against cardboard cartons and wooden crates. We fumbled our way out and went the length of the formal hallway. In the middle there was a bulge, a kind of sunroom projecting over the piazza below."

"It followed the original, except that in this house an elevator shaft was built in on the wall between the sunroom and hallway."

"In a space not much larger than a coat closet," Sam added.

"Apparently it dropped to the foyer below. So this sunroom might be a reception room, in formal terms. You know, like days when a count would receive guests in his dressing gown?" I nodded. "We pushed the brass button, and worried a little about its ability to carry both of us at once."

"It was creaking as it rose, like a wooden cage," Sam added, deflecting any thoughts about his extra weight.

"The outer doors opened and there it was, a highly decorative, wrought-iron cage that fit into the space meant for service stairs in the original plan. Locked inside was the chauffeur we saw driving the old man's limousine. At first we thought he was alive, because he was slouching on the uprights, but his legs were crossed and under his feet there was blood." My spine tingled. Now Sam interrupted again.

"And guess what, Sophie? His necktie wasn't the red one he had on earlier. It was the horsemen!"

"But the tie was slashed through, probably with the same instrument that had stuck the guy through the heart," Jim added.

"What did you do then? Call an ambulance?"

"We still weren't positive there wasn't someone else in the house," Jim continued. "We walked out of the sunroom and slid our backs along the hall walls until we got to the end and the crossroads where, again, a short hallway led to another narrow circular staircase. Again, it was perfectly silent below, no music, no clinking of crockery or banging of bed pans, and no artificial light."

"We took a chance," Sam said. "We took it slowly to the ground floor and kept a lookout for signs of recent activity. We passed the kitchen, dining room, and drawing room, but there were no lights and no voices."

"You were lucky," I said appreciating the risk. "But where was the old man?

"We didn't see him. That's when we phoned in," Sam concluded.

As the ambulance left with the dead chauffeur, Sam told the arriving officers that they needed to find the old man, dead or alive. Another search through the house and then the grounds. No sign of him.

All three of us quietly sipped our drinks. Then, to change the mood of foreboding, "You were both very brave," I said. "It must have been frightening, like a haunted house."

Sam nodded. "I was reminded of this place on Maynard Park, around the corner from my Auntie Nell," he said. "It was tall and skinny and brick, like all the houses on the street, but with a lot of gingerbread trim painted park bench green, and a gardener. I never saw who lived there, but they had to be really old."

"Why old?"

"I never saw kids there."

"Maybe they were being starved to death in the attic," I said, laughing.

"What was your old scary house like?"

"I didn't really have a particular one." I wasn't ready to tell him about my vegetable peddling era. When I was eleven to fifteen my mother and I lived on a little farm outside New London. It had an apple orchard, and Mother planted a few other crops to make up the difference between what my father gave her each month and what we needed. Every

Wednesday during the harvest season I drove our wagon down the street to the corner of Maple Avenue and Ship Street, an overgrown property behind a wrought iron fence so obviously abandoned kept me wondering. I wasn't one for fairy tales, but I had read *The Secret Garden.* I'd stop the wagon and crane my neck. I could see a cupola, and toward the end of October, when the leaves had withered, a few stone columns down one side, suggesting either a porch or a *port cochiere.* There was a single gate facing the sidewalk but it was padlocked. It was ornately designed and perhaps some of the curlicues formed a monogram, but I could never make heads or tails of it. Probably the historical society had information about the house, but back then I never had time to find out. By now some kid probably had written it up for a school project.

As I reminisced, the men were rising to leave and I again congratulated them.

"There's still the old man," Sam said. "All we know now is someone had it in for the chauffeur."

I had unfinished business, too.

A librarian was locking the front doors when I reached them. I gently rapped my knuckles on the glass and it was Mary Kate, thank goodness, who looked up startled and then smiled.

"I have to see something in the archives, I won't take long," I promised. The former colleague looked at her watch.

"I guess I was a little early. Fifteen minutes," she said.

"I need the official death records. And microfiche obits."

"Of course. Year?"

"Years. Start with 1960."

"To . . . ?

"Present." Mary Kate twisted her mouth distastefully. She sighed. "Okay, because it's you, but don't you dare take longer than a half hour. I always take 15 minutes after closing to check around the stacks - just in case someone has fallen asleep back there, or something. You can go leave by the back door with me."

"You're a good friend," I said hastily, waving her to get on with it, get the microfiche.

Ten minutes later I had found Rudolph Urquardt, 55, died March 2, 1979. I whizzed through the obit film to March 3. There was a short write-up. Rudolph was an industrialist with a winter home on an island off Dorado Bay. Two brothers Roland, 53, and Gustav, 24, resided in New York. No more information was given. No wife, no other children, no parents. Gustav was identified as a brother, not step-brother or half-brother. He wasn't any of those to Rudolph. I found that interesting. Either the reporter didn't dig very deep or the three young men were friendly.

Fifteen minutes were up.

"Any luck?" Mary Kate asked when I caught up with her in the lavatory where she was applying fresh lipstick and smoothing her tan knit dress over her rounded hips.

"Not yet. I need something else. A real biography." I explained that I had found Rudolph Urquardt's death announcement and a frustratingly brief notice in the obituary column. Mary Kate nodded and looked at her watch. She went back to the glass-walled reference room and came back with a clip book, *Su-Val*, tucked under one arm and a Florida "Who's Who" tucked under the other. In a few more minutes I had found a slightly longer entry in the latter tome, published in 1960, that Rudolph Urquardt, b. 1926, chemical industrialist, New York City and Florida, was the son of Otto Friedrich Urquardt (b. 1887), an Austrian whose family held a huge amount of wealth in the "old countries." His mother was Beatrice Schneider (1910-1926).

"Sixteen years old! My god!"

Mary Kate came running. "Who?"

"A woman died," I murmured. Mary Kate looked puzzled. "Rudolph's mother apparently died in childbirth – and she was just a child herself." I pointed toward the paragraph and the librarian had a look. "I thought his mother was Otto's second wife. I didn't know about this one."

"It doesn't say what happened to Otto or all that money,"

Mary Kate observed. "'Old countries' usually meant those torn apart by the European wars. Often wealth was confiscated. And often families fled. Today it could be Austria or Poland or Russia, or who knows where?"

"This was after World War I," I noted. But it does tell us Rudolph and Roland had different mothers. It also suggests Otto might have built his chemical industries on residual family wealth. I'm speculating, of course. All we know is that his office was in New York but he had a home in Dorado Bay." She glanced down the page of listings for Roland Urquardt and Gustav Foucault, but there were none. Extrapolating from what he told me, I supposed Roland was in New York in 1979, and Gustav Foucault could be anywhere, because he was no longer a minor. He'd be 24.

"Why didn't I think of looking here in the first place?" I asked myself out loud, turning the "Who's Who" in my hands.

"These were publications of the history society, when society mattered, so people rarely think of them," Mary Kate answered. She looked at me pityingly. "I'm sorry, Sophie, but it's time to go." She picked up the microfiche and headed toward the door saying, "I can't let you stay here and leave when you're done because the alarm will go off."

"We don't want that," I replied, amused at the prospect of Sam's colleagues finding me raiding the town archives for him.

I felt very lucky to be a librarian. We were almost among the first to know how to use the new tools on the Internet. It had been only recently that the consortium was formed to promote and develop standards for what had become known as the World Wide Web. On the way home I kept repeating a refrain from the report of the Foucault plane accident that I simply had to follow up: *The home in Dorado Bay was built by the Tradescants in 1922 but they used it solely to loan to clients and friends. They also died in the war.* Since it said "in" the war, I had to assume they then lived, perhaps were caught, in Europe. That would be an interesting research project some day. But not now.

At home I stuck a low-cal frozen dinner in the microwave and went to the computer and began searching for Gustav and Roland. What a surprise! In what looked like a Lutheran church statewide newsletter published in California in 1975, I found a note that an ordained member, Gustav Foucault had left an assistant pastor position at a church in Los Angeles to start a new fellowship in a valley north of Pasadena. The group was referred to as "pietist." There was no further commentary from the Lutherans, as far as I could tell, but I found a newspaper for Serenidad, the only town in that valley, and a reference to a local historical society there putting its papers in digital form. I found a bit of business on the November 10, 1976, Serenidad town council agenda interesting: "A Lutheran pastor named Gustav T. Foucault has purchased land just beyond the town limits for a church camp and the council discussed annexing the land to be able to levy property taxes. A member reminded the council that church properties were non-profit and therefore not taxable." Someone had argued that it was a phony setup, not a real church. The next item, from the minutes of May 11, 1977, confirmed that the White Angel Farm had filed for non-profit tax status as a religious organization. This was the ranch Deborah had mentioned.

The third interesting item, dated November 12, 1980, recorded that the council had officially banned organized groups from staging anti-war rallies in the park. It referred to a recent event sponsored by White Angel Farm. Gustav continued to be a controversial figure in Serenidad. Was his a band of avenging angels?

I wondered what he was like as a teenager. I hadn't found anything that indicated he was an activist in the 1960s, when other kids were protesting Viet Nam. Probably he was still living at home or at a boarding school. He was quite young when he bought the farm in California. If the Foucaults left him funds that he could spend at age 21, then that would make him free in 1976. He would have had to go on to seminary to be "ordained" and then apparently found his calling in California. Both Rudolph and Roland were alive.

I wondered what they thought of this. Maybe they were proud that he had started a cult and not just joined one.

In order to find Deborah, I needed a map of the area, but probably I'd have to order it from some agency in California. The bell on my microwave timer had sounded a half hour before, so I took my tepid dinner, still in the carton, but on a tray, to my desk, and began to search for more information on Gustav's enterprise.

I completely forgot about watching the six o'clock news, and pretty soon the wind was picking up outside my house. I was too absorbed in finding more about the mysterious rescuer of Deborah Conyers to worry about battening the hatches. By ten, after three more hours zigzagging through the Web, I had established that in 1976 a group of 22 men and women settled on a horse ranch that had been the short-lived hobby of a cowboy movie star. They had established themselves as a religious organization by 1977. According to the occasional local news stories – which never were substantial – members were seen dressed in either a white or brown gown tied at the waist with a rope, and were derided and feared equally when they made appearances in the small town. It was reported that a cult called "The White Angels" tried to organize a non-violent peace rally in Serenidad but gave up when the citizens and especially the local veterans opposed and, reportedly, "shamed" them.

Then they disappeared from the headlines. However, they

prospered selling wheat. Business news publications mentioned White Angel Farm as a producer of high grade wheat for health food products. A few sources noted that Gustav Foucault of White Angel Farm also bought and bred racehorses. Equestrian newsletters commented on the high quality of the stallions. Clearly, by the late 1980s the commune had stopped being a scandal among the surrounding farm families or an embarrassment to the mainstream Lutherans. It ran a prospering business. The members had long since exchanged their sackcloth for denims and leather. They participated in civic events and philanthropies, even sponsoring scholarships for 4-H members who raised horses.

Gustav Foucault rarely was mentioned by name in these gleanings, nor was there reference to the ranch residents' religious activity. I found one tag end that appeared in a recent history of the valley based on oral histories of retired ranchers and farmers. The interviews were conducted by school children in 1992. One of the questions they asked every subject was whether they remembered any bad times, storms, or the drought, or trouble. These were all summarized in one place, the "Trouble" page on the website the kids had designed for this project. A rancher named Jake Lewis had mentioned the white-haired "guru" who was "made fun of" by local people, who ran a commune. He was reputed to be the black sheep of a family of wealthy industrialists who had homes in New York and Florida. The interviewee claimed this guru kidnapped teenagers from their parents, lured them away. The old man was quoted as saying, "They say he died, that the cult dissolved, the kids went away, but I don't think so. I think that was all a sham. Keeps people away. I guess I saw him the other day in the dairy cooperative. Looks like a ghost with that white hair. You could say he is the ghost of Serenidad." I puzzled over the white hair bit because if Gustav was this personage he would be around 43. Was he prematurely gray, or did he wear a wig? What a crazy bunch of brothers these were turning out to be!

The old-timer interviewed apparently hadn't kept up with economic developments on the horse ranch. He didn't mention Gustav or the ranch by name. And why would he single out a memory about a religious "guru" to talk about to kids? The oral historians' request to remember "any bad times, storms, or the drought, or trouble" must have led him to thinking about the trouble surrounding the anti-war demonstrations, the cult leader who kidnapped young people for his "cult," and then he threw in the ghost." Sounded to me like a nasty old man trying to scare these school kids. Beware the cults. Or beware any fringe religions.

The death of Rudolf, second or third-generation industrialist, and conformist to family values, left Roland the lawyer, and Gustav the religious leader turned horse breeder, two very different half-brothers, going their separate ways. These two had a mother but not a father in common. The mother probably had her two boys living as the Foucault family from 1955 to 1962. Roland would have been out of law school. Gustav was only seven when his parents died. Could he have gone to live with his big brother Roland, who might even have been married at that time? When and why did he become interested in religion?

After summarizing what I had found I called Sam's home number but got no answer. What he did with his evenings was nobody's business but his own, but I felt a little annoyed not to have his reaction when I needed it. I slipped the report into my FAX machine and called his number again, pressing the FAX button when his answering machine told me to.

Tuesday, June 23

"Unnhh?"

"Sam, I need to talk to you."

"I'll be in my office at nine."

"It's seven now. Time to get up."

"It doesn't take me two hours to get dressed."

"Take a shower and call me back."

At seven-thirty I told him he had a FAX from me, but went on to explain briefly what I had found out about the "brothers" and what coincidence was on my mind. Officially, there were three unanswered questions about Roland Urquardt's death: Who had motives to kill him? What were the black-jacketed men who visited Deborah interested in? And why hadn't his half-brother Gustav come forward? The coincidence was the arrival of Deborah in California, and my discovery that Gustav owned the White Angel Ranch she had mentioned as her safe haven.

"Why would the much younger brother of the deceased – a half-brother at that – be concerned about a next-door neighbor who was dating a CIA agent watching his mother's island home?" I was being sarcastic to rouse him, but he remained calm.

"This thing is not about Deborah or California," Sam responded. "We have to find out about the old man right here in Dorado Bay. That's the key."

"Okay, maybe that's true. But there's a front door key and a back door key. I want to go and find her," I insisted.

"For all you know, by now she's in Rome or some other damn place."

"I think she's staying in California, and since you don't need me at the island, I'm going to Pasadena tomorrow."

"Okay, Sophie," Sam said, "but don't say I didn't warn you. I'll probably have this wrapped up by the time you get back."

"Ha." I said it that way, though I knew it could be true. I didn't care. I couldn't leave Deborah swinging in the wind.

The man she trusted was two-thirds her age, and not likely to be interested in her good looks. So what was it? I admit: I was curious.

As I packed my bag, I was begrudging the energy I exerted in trying to make Sam into a believer. It might be easier to continue my investigations without telling him anything about what I was doing or what I found. Let him think Deborah was a screwball, a red herring, or whatever.

The phone rang. I ignored it momentarily until the message tape switched on. Through the scratchiness, I recognized Robin's voice. But I couldn't be interrogated now. I let him leave his message. It was his address in Cairo. He repeated it three times. He said he would be leaving Saturday. He'd let me know about the phone number over the weekend. He asked me to call in the next few days to let him know how things were going with the Urquardt case.

Calling from the airport just after two o'clock. I recorded a message on Robin's phone, where it was too early for him to be home Pacific Time: "Don't worry, dear. I'm having a ball. I'm spending quite a lot of time studying historic houses on an island and their vanished families. I might take a little vacation to see my friend Deborah. I'll call you later when we can have a longer conversation." I boarded the jumbo jet half an hour later, hoping for a seat next to a small and quiet sleeper.

It was already ten o'clock when I landed in L.A., and about eleven when my taxicab pulled up in front of the Rose Queen Bed & Breakfast. I had eaten my airplane snack of mini- pretzels in the cab and now brushed the crumbs of salt onto the floor. I was rumpled, but the proprietor was likely used to guests arriving in that condition. The exterior of the house was very tidy, I noted, huffing my way up ten wide, freshly-painted steps. The porch was one of those wrap-around Victorian fancies, with a thousand-and-one spindles along its railings. I paid the driver, who, miracle of miracles, carried my bag to the porch and even rang the bell. As soon as I gave him his tip, he jaunted back down, and drove off as soon as he saw someone coming for the door.

The young woman looked almost as rumpled as I felt. Of course she was slim and blonde, but her blue jeans were overhung with a huge white shirt that had stains on the front, and her blonde hair hung around her collar in jagged hanks. I recognize the shirt as one of those "poet's shirts" you see in casual fashion catalogs. They are designed to make legs look spindly and disguise any puffiness in the midsection. I wondered if she was a poet. After all, this was California.

"Mrs. George?" she asked, red-rimmed glasses perched atop her bangs. Her messy hairdo took on a shine in the porch light. I nodded, and without telling me her name she turned and whistled like a farm boy. A heavy-jawed man with sandy hair appeared out of a dark room and said, "Hi, I'm Bradley Scott," and then marched up a staircase that turned at a double-wide landing. I stepped across the foyer to follow him and the woman stopped me by gently grabbing my arm.

"Mrs. George? Would you like some bedtime herbal tea?"

"How did you know? Thank you, Mrs., uh . . "

"I'm Wendy. I'll bring it to your room, second one on the left." Wendy twirled into what must be the kitchen. There was a glow from a countertop lamp in there. I peeked. Nice, old-fashioned kitchen. Where I had hesitated, I noticed another wide opening to the right, giving me a view of a room that must have been the stage for socialites in the 1920s. Its front half looked like a typical mansion parlor, with tall shutters to cover the bay windows, and furniture upholstered in brocades whose colors I couldn't describe except to say they were pastels that looked almost silver. The other part of the room, reaching deep into the backyard, looked like a conservatory. Sliding doors, the kind that disappear into the walls, were pushed wide enough apart so that I could see the groups of straight-backed chairs and square tables made of bamboo, but structured with the authority of Chinese Chippendale. Perhaps it was meant to be a dining room, but the walls were almost totally obscured by potted palms.

It was all so fresh and lovingly decorated, a welcome contrast from the blood-spattered concrete mansion on the island Sam and Jim had described.

Heading up the stairs to find my room, I passed a wide window on a landing where the stairs turned. Looking out into the dark I could see path lights reflected in a rectangular pool. Tall thin palm trees surrounded the area. I continued the climb, careful not to touch the wallpaper where peasants romped in the pale green and white countryside, the men playing flutes, the girls dancing with floral streamers. When the handrail ran out in a flourish of polished wood, I glanced down the hall to the left and saw Brad waiting for me. He gestured me through a heavily trimmed doorway into a yellow and white guest suite. There were mammoth white roses in a crystal vase on a dark mahogany lady's desk and reflected in the polish. They were real.

"My friend Deborah warned me that I would be treated like the Queen of England," I remarked pleasantly, anxious for the response.

"You have a friend who stayed here?"

Oh, yes. Deborah Conyers. This past week. She knew I was coming to Pasadena and called me to recommend this lovely place. I don't really like big hotels."

"I don't recognize that name. But my wife usually does the checking in. I'm just the handyman," he said with a grin.

"You say she was here this week? I only met one lady who – well, I assume she is about your age?"

"Oh, about. We're both retirees. She looks younger, though." I wondered if she should mention that Deborah was in the company of a man, but it still wasn't clear to me that she was while staying at the B&B. She may have been dropped off by her captors, or escorts, or whoever they were. In fact, this B&B was an educated guess. It did have "Rose" in the name and it was on the parade route.

"Retiree from what, Mrs. George?"

"I was a librarian. But I haven't completely retired. Now I solve . . . " I stopped and smiled coyly, "I write mysteries."

"Oh, so you are going to the Hollywood Screenwriters' Conference, I'll bet."

"That's right," I said, hoping to end that subject.

"Well, then, I'd better let you get your sleep," he said. "It's a pretty brutal three days. I know because I've done that myself." Normally I would have asked him out of politeness what he has written and was it produced, but I just smiled and could see he was disappointed. When he bowed out of the room, I opened the door again and called down the hall, "Bradley, I hope you'll tell me tomorrow about your successes." He just laughed.

Wendy brought my tea on a tray covered with a lace-edged cloth. The pot and cup were mismatched but very delicate china. She had included a tiny honey pot and wooden honey dip, a cloth napkin with butterflies on them, and a brochure for the nearby Huntington Library gardens. It looked lovely, and I wished I could go there, but time was of the essence.

Wednesday, June 24

Wendy looked just as disheveled in the morning, though she was wearing a fresh pink turtleneck sweater and lip gloss. She was quick to pick up the dishes as soon as I had devoured my eggs, bacon, toast and orange juice. She seemed to be rushing me out of the yellow and blue breakfast room, but before I could get up and leave, she returned to fill my coffee cup.

"Thank you. It's very good coffee. In fact, that was something my friend, Deborah Conyers raved about. She stayed here recently."

"Oh? That name isn't familiar, but how recently? You know we bought this place not quite a year ago." Wendy was now drying fruit glasses with paper towels and replacing them on a round painted tray.

"Oh, more recently than that," I replied cheerily. "It was just last week."

"Well, of course I'd remember someone who was here just last week. But that name still is not one I've heard before. She must have stayed somewhere else. There are quite a few bed-and-breakfasts in Pasadena. Most of them quite genteel."

"To tell the truth, she didn't give me the full name, but she said it was 'rose-something,' and yours was the only rose-something in the listings."

"Maybe it's a new one, not in the book yet."

"Maybe," I conceded, but thinking that maybe – probably – Deborah had registered under a different name. With the man. "Oh, silly me," I said. "Well you seem to keep very busy even without my friend and her husband."

"Husband? Oh! We had a couple about your age here last week – for just a night. They were from Florida. The name didn't register."

"Oh? Blonde woman, dark-haired man?"

"I thought he was rather Cuban-looking, actually. He said he was Mr. Jones, as I recall." She looked right at me. "I don't think I ever heard *her* name." I decided to be evasive.

"I'm surprised they stayed just one night. This is such a lovely place."

"Well, they didn't seem to be here for a vacation."

"Oh? Then it couldn't have been Deborah," I lied.

"This woman was very quiet, subdued. He didn't say much either. They hardly talked to each other. I thought they might have been here for a funeral or something like that. Maybe someone was sick and in the hospital."

"Oh, dear. Was she crying?"

"Oh, no. She even smiled a little. But he was so serious. You know – for a Latino. And then a big black limousine picked them up when they left. Naturally, that suggested a funeral."

"It might have been a wedding," I said consolingly.

After a moment of silence she said, "Bradley told me you are here for the writers' conference."

"Well, yes, and I have to do some research this morning. Is there a library nearby?"

"We have a neighborhood branch. It's not a big one."

"I need some help with real estate locations."

"Oh the library is probably not the place. You'll want government records. But come to think of it, the branch library might be able to put you in touch. I can call you a cab." I nodded.

The little library was crowded, so it was clear I wouldn't get a lot of personal attention. On a hunch, I requested the index for the last six months of *L.A. Times*. I couldn't believe how quickly White Angel Ranch came up in my search, or how recently it had been a subject of the real estate gossip section, under the subhead "Plums." I read: "A horse ranch in Angelo Valley that gained some notoriety in the 1980s as a commune of religious fanatics was snapped up by another nonprofit corporation at a surprisingly low price. Agents speculated that its reputation might have caused local buyers to think the estate had fallen apart. We looked. The place is immaculate and in tip top shape. The White Angel Ranch is in fact the renowned source of some of the fastest trotters on the West Coast. The horses are going to Colorado, but we think the property would have been ideal for a developer interested in offering custom homes around an equestrian center."

I did ask for help to locate records that would tell me who the seller was. The woman at the information desk made a phone call. I browsed for ten minutes until she came back with the answer: Gustav T. Foucault. I then asked for maps, and eventually set my eyes on an aerial photograph of Angel Valley, including a town and surrounding ranches. I asked for a magnifying glass. An assistant took me to a corner where there was one mounted on a lectern. It was about the size of a dinner plate. Manipulating it over the map I could see what was labeled the White Angel Ranch. It was big. There was a long drive to a rambling house that continued past the stables and some other white buildings, then abruptly turned and ended at a little house. I could imagine any minute a black limousine approaching, and the dark driver pulling Deborah out by the arm.

"I wish I could see what's going on there right now," I said aloud, not intentionally. The library assistant was still beside me, standing with hand on hip, one leg crooked, and chewing gum.

"Come back in a few years," she said smartly. I made

some notes on my steno pad and handed the map back to her.

"If I'm still among the living," I replied and gave her a big toothy smile.

Back at the Rose Queen Inn, I sipped Wendy's herbal tea and considered my options. There really weren't any. I was not going to try driving 30 miles on labyrinthine roads in California traffic. I could get a taxi to get me there, and arrive at the door as a prospective buyer who didn't know the property was in escrow. But who would believe I was serious? Anyway, they probably wouldn't talk to anyone without an agent. Maybe I could get one. I called to Wendy through the doorway to the kitchen.

"Do you know a real estate agent I could talk to?"

"Are you buying a place? How nice! In Pasadena?"

"Out in the country someplace. I'm thinking of buying a ranch." I watched the young woman's expression change from surprise to concern.

"A ranch? To live on? Alone?"

"Well, I'd have hands."

"Ranch hands?" Now I think she was trying to remain composed and not burst out laughing at my Hollywood Western terminology.

"Well, do you know an agent?"

"It's hard to say where to start," she finally responded. "I could put you in touch with the woman who sold us this place."

"Do you think she knows ranches?"

"Probably not. But, Mrs. George, are you sure you want to live like that here in California? For one thing, a ranch is a huge responsibility. For another, one is bound to be expensive."

"How expensive?"

"Oh, twenty million, perhaps. At least."

Then I realized how ludicrous I must seem, a woman of my age, all by myself, inquiring of a small business owner how I should go about buying multimillion-dollar real estate. Wendy surely had enough of a head on her shoulders to see I was a fraud – or plain dotty.

"Okay. Let me tell you really what I really need. I need someone credible who can go with me to a ranch that is – or was – for sale. I need to find out if my friend is there."

"The friend – who was *here*?"

"Yes. Deborah was lured away from the Houston Airport by two men and brought here. She called me from there and again from a pay phone when she was staying here. She thinks she is being rescued, but she's actually in real danger. When she told me she was staying at a Pasadena B&B with the word "rose" in its name, and it was on the street the Rose Bowl Parade goes down, I – that's why I'm here." I looked

Deborah in the eye and could see she remained skeptical.

"Where does the ranch come in?"

"She told me she was going into protection at a religious commune named White Angel Ranch. It's apparently a well-known horse ranch northeast of Pasadena. I saw a map of it at the library. The problem is, she sounded happy, and maybe you don't believe me, but I can tell you she has reason to be frightened. For one thing, the ranch has been sold. The seller is the son of a gang godfather type. He's the guru, and she thinks he's rescued her from – oh, well, it's a long story." I put my head between my hands."

"I don't know, Sophie, if a Realtor would go for this. First of all, it's been sold. A Realtor would know that. Even if the Realtor pretended not to know it has been sold, it could be construed as an invasion of privacy. Let me think a minute." She went into the kitchen and brought out some hot muffins. "Look. I am new at this B&B business. A year ago I was a banking executive when we bought this house. I was aiming for the top, before I became pregnant. I lost the baby and was told that I would have to stop working so hard if I wanted to have one." She paused. "We could keep the house only by running it as a B&B, so I'm working just as hard, but at least I'm at home." I was a bit embarrassed to hear this private confession, but knew there must be a purpose to her telling me. I waited.

"I know real estate."

"Ahhh." My whole face smiled.

I was very tempted to let Sam know what I had accomplished. I was even more interested in what he might be doing in my absence. Had the necktie revelation amounted to anything? What about Hank's CIA connection? Finally I talked myself into calling.

"Captain Rueben Samuels," he answered in his efficient manner. Apparently he was on call.

"Sam, it's Sophie. I'm calling from California. I'm wondering how things are going."

"You're missing all the fun. An hour ago we got word a body was found washed up on the beach on another island north of the war games retreat. Some teenage kid fooling around in a boat found it. Jim is on the scene, I'm central command. He just called me to confirm it's an old man. Really old. He appears to have drowned."

"Our old man?" I asked, my tummy aflutter. I hate it when kids are the ones to find dead bodies, even of animals.

"There are no marks on his body, no identification. If it is the old man, you know as well as I do there is no one to claim him. His two sons are dead and his chauffeur, too."

"Was there a necktie around . . .?" As soon as I started to ask that question I knew it was silly. Jim would have said something.

"He was wearing pajamas. It looks like he wandered down to the dock and fell."

"Wander? Could he walk?"

"Well, that's a good question," Sam snapped back.

"Any more news about Hank?"

"All we know is that he had a family – an ex-wife and child – who live in New Jersey somewhere. Pretty well, I was told. I would guess she got any salary he made."

"But no one knows what he was doing here?"

"No one is telling. We told them about Urquardt, of course. They didn't comment."

"Did you mention Deborah?"

"I mentioned he had a girlfriend and that she has left town."

"And they didn't comment."

"That's right."

I briefed him on what I was doing and who my new sidekick was, and said I'd call after we visited the ranch where Deborah said she'd be staying. He grunted what might have been approval or disinterest. I went to bed feeling restless and all the more so knowing I needed a good night's sleep. Finally, I tiptoed down the hall to the staircase and listened. There were noises in the kitchen. I went down the stairs and found Bradley sitting at the kitchen table with a Dagwood sandwich and a beer.

"Mrs. George! Is something wrong?"

"I can't sleep. I wondered if I could have some Sleepytime tea."

"How about some Christian Brothers brandy?" he asked. That sounded good. Somehow, monks' wine seemed less dangerous. It also seemed appropriate to my chore tomorrow: I would be protected by an older cult. Bradley warmed some water in the teakettle and poured it slowly on top of a good two inches in a cut glass snifter.

"So, tell me about your project, Sophie George. Are you close to finished? Have an agent?"

"I don't have an agent yet, and I have no idea if I am close to finished," I told him. "As Wendy will tell you, if she hasn't already, I lied to you about why I am here."

"No, she didn't say." I thought then that maybe she didn't want him to know she was going to help me.

"I'm trying to locate a long lost friend," I said, and left it at that. "What about you? I got the impression you are a real writer."

"I am. Unfortunately, I'm working for an ad agency."

"What's unfortunate about that?"

"I have to lie, too," he said. I had to laugh.

"And the screenwriting?"

"Back burner. I studied screenwriting at UCLA and was the star of my class. I worked at it until my money ran out – money left to me by my grandfather – finished a couple and hired an agent who sold one that's never been produced.

The other just didn't appeal to anyone. So I put it all aside and got a day job, intending to take it up when I was making enough money. However, writing all day burns me out."

"I'm sorry. Maybe the day will come. In retirement, perhaps." He smiled weakly, asked me if I wanted more, and I said no, this would do the trick, and I padded up the stairs.

Thursday, June 25

"Mrs. George!" Wendy rushed out of the kitchen when she heard me coming down the stairs.

"Call me Sophie, please," I said, smiling in anticipation of a great day as sleuthing partners.

"Look!" Wendy shoved the morning paper in front of my face and pointed to the headline: SERENIDAD LANDMARK A CHARRED RUIN. My eyes quickly traveled down the column. Arson was suspected. The local fire fighters thought the fire might have started with electrical wiring dating back to the 1930s; but fragments of rolled blankets suggested a deliberate act. Arson would be plausible, since the property had been sold and the place was going to be demolished anyway. "Some developer in a hurry," a resident and council member of Serenidad was quoted as saying. The compound had been condemned.

"It's on TV, too!"

"Oh, no! Deborah! Was there a body?" Deborah's safety was my first concern. But certainly the headlines would have mentioned something so grisly.

"Not that they're talking about," Wendy said. "But they'll have to sift through the mess before they know for sure."

We didn't look out of place at the scene with notepads conspicuously peeping out of our handbags. We had walked from where Wendy parked her Volvo, a quarter mile down a side road, to reach the prominent arch at the main ranch entrance, but found the place fenced off with orange construction webbing and yellow caution tape. Inside the perimeter a couple of small earth movers were busy clearing the cooling debris as men in uniforms moved around them with hoses spraying water and foam. A few TV trucks had pulled up in a circle on a wide part of the road where a secondary gate opened onto the lane to the stables. We walked up to one of the reporters who were scribbling away.

"Do you know, did everyone get out?" Wendy asked.

"All humans, a far as we know," he answered in collegial fashion. "About eight racehorses died, though. Seems odd. They should have been led out. Pathetic."

"Looks like arson then?" I asked, squinting against the sun that was a bright ball behind the smoke. The young man shrugged and turned his back on us. We were on our own. As soon as it became known to the police that we had no press passes, we were told to keep our distance. It was a public highway. We could hike along there – just keep moving. We went up one way and then back down, pausing to query several men, some from the sheriff's investigation team and others apparently volunteers, but just got impatient stares and shakes of the head.

"Let's go into town," Wendy suggested. We walked back to the car and headed into Serenidad, stopping at the first intersection where there was a gas station, snack store, and bathrooms. There was a swarm of kids standing outside the entrance, and the parking lot was full. We pushed our way in and stood eyeing the place. There were lines at each register, mostly kids. School was just out. Wendy went back outside and around a corner of the building where she could call Bradley and let him know where we were. After pulling myself together in the not-too-filthy restroom, I wandered over to the wall that was all cooler and mostly beer, eventually picking out two bottles of orange juice. The place had almost cleared. One young clerk was bracing herself on the ice cream freezer with two thin stiff arms, gazing across the aisle toward the glass entrance. She wore a sweatshirt with a school mascot on the front, the sleeves pushed up to her elbows. I thought she was a teenager, but up close I could see she had wrinkles at the corners of her mouth and eyes.

"Quite a bit of excitement around here today," I remarked.

"Yeah. End of a era."

"What do you mean?"

"That place, well, it's got a history."

"Oh? Movie stars?"

"No. Cults or something."

"I see. Charles Manson?"

The young woman looked blank, so I explained to her about the Charles Manson case, and the clerk, who must have been in her twenties, obviously didn't think it merited explaining. She looked bored as she shifted from one foot to another.

"What kind of cult was it?"

"I don't know, just heard it was a cult."

"Did the members come here?"

"I guess. I never saw anyone that said he was from a cult." She gave me a deadpan look that perhaps was meant to inspire a chuckle, and I decided to play along with her."

"No long dresses or turbans?"

"Nope."

"Black jackets?"

"Lots of those, but they are the tattooooed bikers," the girl explained, her eyes purposely big to match the extra "o's" in her speech. I had to wonder when the girl saw the tattoos if their arms were in jacket sleeves, but the question was prissy and pointless.

"I meant that I'm interested in knowing if you have seen any Italian Mafia types," I said. "Seriously." The girl looked up at me sideways with slitty eyes.

"You from around here?"

"Oh, no. I was just getting carried away." The girl looked blank once more. I turned, hiding my embarrassment. Sam had told me that I blushed when I was caught out of my usual mental composure.

Wendy and I got home just in time to watch the TV news, but there was nothing new about the fire or its survivors. Bradley insisted on taking us to their favorite Italian restaurant. It was a joke (the black jacketed "Italians") and an antidote to our aura of gloom. I did call Sam, using my calling card, and told him how my investigation had ended. The good news was that he didn't say I told you so. The next chapter – or end – of Deborah's story would just have to wait for further developments.

THIRD WEEK

Friday, June 26

Halfway back to Florida, my mind was in turmoil. Wendy had offered to let me stay on without paying for the room. I did want to understand more about the ranch, but when the morning papers again did not mention bodies, I knew there was little likelihood Deborah had been in the fire. But where would she be now? It was time to consult with Sam. It seemed, though, that there were no straggling ends here in California that connected to anything in Florida, except, of course, that Gustav Foucault was the owner of the ranch. And where was he? Then I wondered about the buyers of the ranch property. Would they know anything about Gustav, for example, have telephone numbers for reaching him, wherever he was? Darn! Why didn't I think about that earlier, before I left LAX? As soon as I got home I would have to call Wendy and ask if she could find out how to reach them.

My thoughts drifted back to Roland, the old man, and the island. I replayed the scene, ostensibly a paint ball session, and most likely a cover for deliberate murder. No body had ever been found. No one was being held or even arrested. Where could the men have bought guns like the ones they had? Did you have to have a license for paint guns? That was another fact to check, though it seemed unlikely. You probably got them at a toy store. The real gun was something else to check on. No body, no bullet, but you could figure out what guns looked like paint guns. Unless of course an ordinary gun and a silencer were used.

After changing planes in Houston at about 3:00 p.m., we were stuck on the ground in a lightning storm. They wouldn't let us off the plane because we had already rolled onto the runway when the change of flight plans came through. Two and a half hours later, frustrated, hungry, and grumpy, we flew along the Gulf of Mexico, skirting the remaining storm, and landed in Tampa at 8:30 p.m. By nine I was out the airport door, but Dorado Bay was still an hour's taxi ride away. I fell asleep on the smooth highway, and woke only as we drove over the gorgeous bay bridge with its cables shining like a row of angel wings. From Angel Ranch to Angel Home. And me an agnostic.

As soon as I got inside my snug condo, I checked my messages. I had four, three from Robin, one from Sam. I played Sam's first. He sounded jovial.

"I'm just back from New York, Sophie. Can't talk until later, but I've got a lot to tell you." Click.

"I wish I could say the same," I muttered. Nonetheless,

I dialed Sam's number. No answer. I quickly put the receiver back in the cradle, wondering if I should have let it ring longer, or if he was out. Then I played Robin's messages. One asked me to call "immediately after hearing this message," plain and simple. The second one stated he was really worried that I wouldn't be in touch before he had to leave for Egypt. The third, left about when I was stuck at the Houston airport, asked why I didn't bother to check my messages, and why didn't I buy a mobile phone, and why didn't I leave addresses of where I'd be when I traveled. He was clearly angry and frustrated. Then I realized with great shame that I had been within miles of where he lived and hadn't tried to see him. It was still before his bedtime back in the Pacific Time zone, so I called.

"Yep, it's me, Mom. So I'm not an orphan yet?"

"How did you know it was me," I asked, astonished.

"I have caller I.D." he said, and explained that my number had come up on a tiny screen. I thought that was a wonderful idea. Too bad Deborah hadn't had that kind of phone when the men called her that morning. We'd be a lot further along.

"So how was your trip?"

"It was quick," I said, "but fun." I hated to lie to my own son, but I couldn't tell him I had been in Los Angeles. I decided to tease was a good way out of this: "We went clubbing and hooked up with a couple of younger men. It's amazing what wearing diamonds does for the ego."

"Mom! I know you are jerking me around. What gives?"

"Oh, I just wanted to satisfy your worrying."

Thankfully, that put him at ease and we talked a bit about his Cairo assignment and would I be interested in riding a camel. I declined but said maybe I could make a trip to L.A. to see him when he got back in six months.

As I was crawling into bed, rather happy, I realized it was Friday night. I had missed my usual dinner date with Sam. I had chosen flights to make sure to be home, but the storm held us up. My only excuse was, stuck on the runway, I had no way to have called him anyway. No mobile phone. What was all his news? It took a while to get to sleep.

Saturday, June 27

I overslept. That hardly ever happens, but it spared me several extra hours of worrying about what Sam was up to. I had just finished getting unpacked, showered, and dressed for the day when Sam called. I explained what happened to my flight.

"Let's have lunch," he said. "We have something to celebrate."

"I just ate breakfast," I said, "but come on over here and

I'll make you a sandwich." I wasn't sure what I had in the refrigerator, so when he insisted we go out to my favorite "old Florida" hotel, I said yes, and agreed to meet him there. It was on the beach near his office, the library, the art museum, and not far from historic Front Street. The setting would be perfect if there was to be an unraveling of this crime.

Sam greeted me warmly in the plush foyer of the recently refurbished Hotel Conquistador. It had taken millions to redo the place in the traditional way with original materials instead of faux everything. It looked splendid. The hostess led us to a table Sam had reserved by a tall narrow window looking onto a garden of ferns with splashes of brilliant colors mixed in, and a view of the beach lined with supple palms lazily waving their fronds in the breeze. Peacocks wandered into the courtyard beside us and displayed their finery every once in a while. The windows were closed, or we might have been startled by their shrieking.

"Well?" I asked after we had ordered drinks.

"Well! We got the CIA to fess up and let us in on Hank's operations. At least enough to figure out what's happening on the island. Or what's happened. I think it's over."

"What's over?"

"The killing games. The paint ball tournaments were a cover for what the criminal activity was. What we saw that day was an assassination."

"Have they found bodies?" I was remembering how they

deftly removed the dead man to the trunk of a limousine. "Who was killing who – or whom?"

"I have to hand it to you, Sophie. You were absolutely right. It was a corporation, but also a sort of brotherhood, a group of men working together under Otto Urquardt. Their business was to kill men on contract for revenge."

"Just men?" I thought of all the marital murders I've heard about.

"Men who fought in wars. These revenge killings were, you might say, an eye for an eye. It started in Germany, even before the Second World War, with the old man in charge. The name was originally Eberhardt."

"The old man in the wheelchair?"

"Otto Eberhardt was a young man when he set this up to settle scores. He was a chemist, and immigrated to the States in 1930, changing his name so it sounded Scots. When his friends or family members back home were killed, he tracked the killers down, as many as he could. As you know, in those days, the loss of a man was the loss of an income for a family forever. Sometimes these killers looted homes. You've heard these stories.

"Too many." But I thought to myself that my ancestors had nothing to loot.

"Eventually, the CIA thinks, about when Otto retired, he set up a false corporation and began to charge fairly large sums of money to do this for anyone else who was hell-bent on paying back for their loss. A chemical company was a good way to hide the means to kill. They made poisons. His son Rudolph also was a chemist. Roland helped through his connections specializing in martial law, with access to military information. But by that time they weren't particular about sides."

"Then Rudolph died."

"Yes. Roland continued his work as a lawyer, but other men had been recruited to take over the chemical company. The paintball was just somebody's odd idea that happened to work." It seemed safer, and cheaper. The chemical company was sold.

"But what about Roland? Was he still involved when he died?"

"That's where it gets murky."

"But he had a tie around his neck when he was found."

"Yes. That would suggest there had been a falling out with the brotherhood. I didn't tell you earlier, because we were trying to make a hypothesis that would stick, but the boxes unloaded at his house were archived files, personal records, the fruits of research on individuals who had military careers. They probably were for locating men to kill. But why he had them delivered to his house, we still can't quite figure. He might have planned to destroy them, or he might have planned to contact the families and make restitution."

"Do you know where they came from?"

"We found some boxes with the same kind of information at the old house on the island. It could be that they all were stored there, but also at the company. Who was moving them out we don't know for sure. Your neighbor just happened to see one delivery. My guess is that the old gang was breaking up. Maybe they were fighting each other.

By now our food had come and although I'd ordered from the list of appetizers, I didn't feel like eating. We should be celebrating, as Sam said, because the case was cracked. It's just that there were so many loose ends. One being Deborah's disappearance.

"Let's go for a ride," Sam said when he had finished.

"Why not?" I excused myself to tidy up and when I returned to the table Sam had paid the check and was standing near a potted palm and talking on his mobile phone.

"Purcell," he told me when he had hung up. "He said he was thinking about the night he took you to explore his basement, and it gave him an idea. We're going to take a ride, but not the romantic one I had planned."

I was a little surprised at the suggestion of anything romantic, but didn't contradict him. I dutifully followed him to the police car.

Sam flashed his credential at the gatekeeper who was also dressed in the uniform of the police department. Apparently the force had taken over the entire island compound. Sam drove on to where Jim was standing with his hand in the air to catch our attention. We parked alongside several other cars, two of them big Chevrolets that the City Council has approved for the chase squad last year. There had been quite a fuss about it. As one of my neighbors put it, "Why get an expensive car if all you're going to do with it is bang it up?"

Jim silently led us to a side entrance of one of the newer houses. We were on a landing somewhere between the main floor and the basement. Halfway down several wide, carpeted steps, so unlike the narrow and dark ones in his own house, Jim pointed to the end of the low-ceilinged recreation room where doors opened onto a beachside patio. Three other policemen were hunkered around the opening of an enormous fire pit. One of them was pulling out ashes. He was dumping them into a wheelbarrow, and they were periodically emptying the barrow into black plastic bags.

"Do we know for sure?" Sam asked, not having to go into detail.

"Doc was down here and got a sample. We're waiting for his report. We're finding belt buckles, though."

"Have you finished the searches of all the houses?" Sam asked.

"Yes, and the boathouse. You will be interested in what we found there." After a few more exchanges of what to do next and who would be in touch with Sam, Jim told us to follow him down the road to the south end of the island where the big house was. We got out of our cars. I was hoping we could tour the house, but Jim beckoned us to a path that led from the drive down the slope to the shore. We stopped when we got to the boathouse. Unlocking the door, Jim said he figured, based on architectural styles, the boathouse had been built and rebuilt over 70 years as storm damage required. There was electricity now, and when he threw the switch we saw two berths, one with a fairly new cabin cruiser about the size of my condo. The other berth was empty. He held my elbow and guided me around the edge to an exhibit of photographs hanging on the wooden wall. Some of them showed storm damage, confirming his deductions. Among those were three photos of a vintage yacht. In one it looked brand new and shiny, circa 1940. In the next it was badly beaten up, presumably by a storm. In the third it was partially restored.

"It looks like the one Frank Dobbs took his last sail on," Sam said.

"And here's something else," Jim said, pointing to an empty space along the opposite wall.

"What? I don't see anything," I said.

"Right. There's no small boat here," Sam said, catching on right away. "There should be a rowboat at least, something functional."

"That's what I think. I have an idea. Do you want to hear it?" Jim's eyes sparkled.

"Yeah, go ahead."

He led us out of the boathouse, down to the sand, and we sat side by side on a log that had served as a mooring. The waves were gently lapping the shore about five feet away. I had the impulse to take my shoes off and wade, or go shelling. Forget killing. But I listened.

"I think the chauffeur knew the old man was going to get it between the eyes – or some such thing, probably more subtle. Judging him to be in his late fifties, I expect over the decades of his service – for we did find out he had been employed here since 1956 – he and the old man had grown fond of one another. It's my guess – we also saw quite a bit of sloughing off of sand, almost trenches, like a boat had been dragged out here – that he, the chauffeur, decided to get the old man off the island and hide him somewhere." By then Jim had walked over to a place where clearly there was the last evidence of a trench made by a heavy elongated object.

"But was caught?" Sam asked.

"Murdered and put in the elevator cage. All they had to do was continue with the job of getting the old man, who was already in the boat, out into deep water and then shove him over the edge. The killer could easily swim back."

"No evidence of a wheelchair?" I asked, breaking my silence.

"It's in the car trunk. He must have carried the old man in his arms."

"Did he have a name?"

"Just plain William Smith. I suspect it was an alias."

After our tour was over and we were on our way out, Sam's phone rang again and it was Jim saying they had heard from the lab that there were human remains in the ashes of four fire pits along the beach, in fact accounting for about half of each sample. Sam drove the long way back to town, taking the road that connected all the keys, starting at the top where I showed him where Monty and I used to live. When we crossed the bridge at Old Harbor and headed back up the main street leading to Bridgewater, I was truly depressed.

"Want to stop for a nightcap?" Sam asked, sensing my mood from my silence. He really could be sweet. I shook my head.

"But thanks. It's been a long, hard day."

"Are you thinking of your husband? Sam asked.

"Oh, no. Further back than that."

"I know what you mean," Captain Rueben Samuels, my fellow lapsed Jew, admitted. "Makes one, I don't know, maybe want a second coming of Moses."

"Yes," I agreed, smiling. "Or at least light some candles."

As we pulled into the neighborhood we noticed a black car parked in Deborah's driveway. My heart began beating rapidly. Sam pulled to my corner and watched in the rear view mirror. He could see someone sitting in the car. He moved forward slowly until we got into my carport. As quietly as we could, we got out and positioned ourselves in two folding chairs I keep near my front porch. Unlike Deborah, who was a people-watcher, I use my chairs for weeding along my hedges under the windows, one to sit on, and the other for my equipment. We said nothing, but watched until finally Deborah came out of her house, arms loaded with something we couldn't make out in the dark. She looked up and the man waiting in the car got out and helped her put her burden in the trunk. She got into the passenger seat.

Sam got up and walked quickly to the man at the back of the car, and I heard him introduce himself and flash his badge. The man began to get into the car, but Deborah got out. At that point I ran over to greet her with a hug. She cried and let me lead her back to my living room. Sam and the man followed. We all sat. I offered drinks. They shook their heads, but Sam asked for bourbon straight, and they finally consented to a glass of wine. I had one, too. It was the bottle Wendy had tucked into my tote bag, saying it was a new blend her father, a vintner, was experimenting with. He calls it "Opulence." It seemed to go with the huge diamond ring Deborah was wearing.

"What brought you back?" I asked her.

"Where should I start?" Deborah asked herself. "Well,

this is Gustav Foucault, Roland's step-brother. He owns property here in Dorado Bay." Did they know about the drowning?

"He's the spiritual leader I told you about, Sophie," she went on, glancing upwards at him with a pretty smile. He nodded politely but looked scared to death, white and haggard, his graying ponytail coming out of its band. He was dressed in jeans, but, I noticed, a very expensive-looking shirt. His boots looked like Robin's childhood dream: French calf with elaborate overlays of kangaroo, embroidered, and with his initials.

"We just came to get some of my things," she continued, "as I am staying in California for a while, as I told you over the phone, Sophie."

"I know about the fire," I said, keeping all emotion out of my voice. This stopped her smile in its tracks. "What on earth happened?" She was speechless, but Gustav, probably to protect her after all, began to fill in the details.

"My ranch caught on fire. It doesn't matter. We're going to rebuild it."

"But I thought you sold it!" I exclaimed. My voice was rising in volume and pitch and Sam, seated next to me on the sofa, patted my arm.

"How do you know all this?" Deborah asked.

"I went looking for you," I said, probably sounding annoyed.

"I had just sold it to one of my other corporations," Gustav explained.

"One of your *other* corporations?"

"Well, I should say, one of the companies my family owns."

"West Coast Holdings?" Sam asked.

"How did you know *that*?" the strangely old-looking young man asked, furrowing his brow, his jaw slack.

"We've had quite a lot of excitement around here concerning your family," Sam said. "What do you know about it?"

I guess Gustav saw in Sam's eyes that he wasn't going to get away without coming clean about the family business and whatever he knew about Roland's death. He said, "I am aware that my half-brother was murdered. I know who did it. At least I know how it came about." He then told us in as brief a condensation as he could – and it was difficult – that as soon as he had come of age he took his trust fund and became a Lutheran minister, for no rational reason other than he was a pacifist and had no obvious talents.

"My dad was a bad artist, and I wasn't going to follow in his footsteps. I met a Lutheran minister who spoke at my school, and he was a pacifist. That was my earliest influence. I expected all Lutherans were so inclined."

"That's understandable. But how did you wind up raising horses? "I didn't tell him that I had traced his young life through seminary and beyond.

"When I answered a calling to a large church in California, my colleagues were aware of my wealth, and some of the lay leaders wanted me to fund the revival of the Ministerium that had once governed all Lutheran pastoral work. I didn't like that idea. I wanted a simple religion, dedicated to world peace. I believe in the powerful influence of committed laity, but I had very specific goals and did not want to be sidetracked into administration or development and all that superficial 'friend-making.' At that time, I had all the money I needed to do exactly what I wanted with my ministry. Eventually, one of my concerns was how to make my money last without getting involved with the family. A few of my congregation who followed me in forming the religious retreat had ranching experience, and we all agreed on what our most important work was to be. The ranch became the economic engine for our activities."

"But you and Deborah – how did you meet?" I asked, impatient with this piety bordering on arrogance. He represented much of what I disliked about modern churches. Noble cause, and then compromise.

"What about your brothers?" Sam demanded. He was getting annoyed at this skirting of the issues. The pastor put his hands up and signaled he was coming to that.

"Remember, I'm a Foucault. I wasn't part of the Urquardt ideological inheritance. It's true that my step-brother Roland looked after me when Mother and Father died, but I wanted nothing to do with West Coast Holdings then."

"Let me fast forward," Sam said. "We know about their work as avengers, locating and executing 'war criminals.' Is that why you were a declared pacifist?"

"I spent some vacation time in Dorado Bay with the Urquardts. Roland took me there. I figured it out. I confronted Roland. I told him I could see how easy it was to get away with kidnapping soldiers in countries where there was no infrastructure. Usually they had been separated from their families for a long time."

"What did he say?" I wondered.

"He didn't defend it. He just told me I should do what I wanted to do. He said he believed in me. That meant a lot."

"I still don't understand how you and Deborah met," I said.

"Roland came to me about five years ago. His father, Otto, was old. The newer members had been running things more like a business. It had lost its soul."

I cringed at this. Deborah was looking confused. Gustav seemed relieved to be telling us his side of the story.

"Roland said he wanted to bring the business to a close. I owed him a great deal so I offered to cooperate. I still had my mother's shares."

"She knew what the business was?"

"Mother told me that's why she divorced Urquardt."

"Then we stepped in, and it's over. So why are *you* here?" Sam asked Gustav.

"There's more to explain first. Roland and I agreed that we should bring in the CIA. I did it, communicating as a clergyman from California. I didn't tell them about family ties, I only told them that, as a pacifist, I had heard from someone in Florida that this vigilante retribution was going on. They sent Hank to scope it out. He quickly found out that a small core group of followers were preparing to get rid of the old man and take over, perhaps move it to some other location."

"How did Hank plan to stop that from happening?"

"We were very careful in communicating. We had carrier pigeons. Hank contacted Roland and sometimes they met on boats at sea. Roland knew when and where another target had been located and sent a message to Hank. Hank notified his colleagues and they intervened. The members of the corporation didn't figure it out for a long time."

"Until the pipeline was going dry," Sam grimly observed.

"You might say that. They suspected they were being watched by CIA. They got the idea to bring the paint ball into it. Then one member noticed some of the archived records were gone. There had to be an insider involved. That's when Roland started to deep sea fish a lot. They spotted him with Hank Norris on a boat."

"He was fishing," Sam punned. Gustav nodded and simultaneously put his arm around Deborah's shoulders. "When Hank stopped messaging Roland, Roland called me, and I called our CIA contact in Washington. They figured he was dead and that somehow Otto's men had found out about his existence, his surveillance."

"But what did they say about the suicide? We couldn't see any evidence of murder," Sam contended.

"Of course not," I chimed in. "The CIA got there first and removed the evidence."

"No," Gustav answered. "The CIA was not on the scene immediately. It's just that Hank's work routine was very well established, he had tremendous self-discipline, and he would have been in touch if he felt his effectiveness was being compromised by anything, even personal problems. They were certain he wouldn't have committed suicide. So they waited. They wanted to see who showed up at the funeral and afterward. No one did, not even his kid. That's when they sent the 'brother' down."

"But I thought he had financial problems," I said, thinking that might be on Deborah's mind.

"Not exactly," Gustav replied. "He somehow managed to drain his accounts quickly and made it look like he was about to go on the dole."

"And this man pretending to be a brother couldn't tell me

the truth!" Deborah declared sulkily.

"The CIA played along with the suicide idea to keep everyone at bay until they found out more. Roland was the one who could come and go on the island. He reported to us that his father seemed to be failing. He suspected they were drugging him. He was walking a fine line from then on, playing their game, feeding them false information, pretending to fail to locate targets or run into legal snafus. He had friends in the group, of course, thinking he would lead them to safety. But the ones who stepped forward to take over Otto's role became impatient and began to watch Roland's house."

"Ah, yes," Sam said. "And did they see the boxed archives arrive?"

"Could be. But after that one delivery, he had them stored in his other houses in the neighborhood."

"Who finally found out?" Sam asked.

"How did they find out?" was my question.

"The two members who came to see Deborah had noticed all the Shady Lane FOR SALE signs. They were aware of Hank's girlfriend, coincidentally Roland's neighbor, rented her house from the same company. They quickly found out Roland owned Shady Lane. They just kept watching those houses, and that night he walked out of one of them and took a walk to the pond."

"But even then the CIA didn't tell EBPD." Sam was

rubbing his hands together, looking at his shoes. I looked at my hands, my wrinkled fingers, age-spotted wrists, my wedding ring. It was a small diamond, the largest Monty could afford at the time. I'd always worn it, even though he offered to replace it with a bigger one. I guess I wasn't listening to Sam. I didn't want to hear the depth of his pain. He felt so left out, so over-the-hill.

But then Gustav said something very helpful. "With Otto gone, you and the CIA will have to go after the members of the organization. They used false names here, but most live along the East Coast, and I can get that information. Let's meet tomorrow."

"Good," said Sam. His smile was tentative. He turned to Deborah. "And what's your story?"

I walked into the kitchen and got us some water and wine. I gave the water to Sam. He looked up at me momentarily with pursed lips. Deborah took a sip of wine and then started talking rapidly. She was near tears.

"Of course, I didn't know Hank was CIA. He kept that from me. I didn't know Roland had a father – or much of anything about him. I was the complete dumb blonde, I guess," she said, looking Sam in the eye. She turned to me. "You know I would have come to you with any suspicions, Sophie." I nodded, though I wasn't sure. We hardly knew each other at the time all this began.

"How did you and Gustav come together?" I asked.

"Remember the plane ticket in the flowers?" I nodded. "I didn't know at the time that Gustav even existed – but he sent it. Roland had asked him to get me out of there if anyone killed him. And we weren't even really friends. I suppose he did it for Hank."

"But he had you remove the pigeon" I recalled. "Who did you give it to?"

"I killed it with some poison Roland told me was in his shed. I put it in his food after I got home. I buried him in my backyard. Believe me, it was the hardest thing I ever had to do."

"I hope nobody with kids moves in and they start digging," Sam said.

"We have rules against that," Deborah reassured him. "This is an age-restricted community." Now I wondered about the fate of Roland's dog Scout.

Sunday, June 28

Deborah looked refreshed and almost happy when I went over to her house to help her pack and arrange for the house to be cleaned after she left. Gustav had left for California after meeting with Sam. She was flying back to join him and become one of the pacifist activists. She was excited about her future, building a new compound with the group. She imagined a kind of barn-raising. Fellowship. Purpose.

"How do you think the fire happened?" I asked her.

"It was my fault. There was no heating in the cottage. They brought me food on a tray. On the second day I asked for some bourbon. That was my downfall. By the time I'd had my fourth drink and no one had come to see me, I decided I had to escape."

She described the atmosphere, the cement floors, scored to look like large tiles, the wood-slatted rocking chairs and matching sofas. Only the cushions made them comfortable. There was one Hollywood style lounge chair, and she tried to sleep there, but it was uncomfortably cold. She pulled blankets off the bed and made a kind of sleep sack. There was nothing to read, not one magazine. The alcohol was fuzzing her vision, but she poured another inch from the bottle parked on the floor. If it put her to sleep, all the better. She didn't even know what time it was.

"I began to doubt Gustav. I remembered that when the black car arrived for me at the B&B, my escort made sure I got out of the house without the opportunity to tell the proprietors goodbye, to mention where I was going. He opened the back door and introduced me to 'the Pastor' with whom I would share the leather seat. This 'Pastor' was very sweet to me all the way to the ranch. He talked softly and told me I would be all right in a little while. But he didn't tell me about Hank being with the CIA or that he was murdered. I had a million questions. And then he left me in the cottage for a couple of days without coming to see me."

"I kept drinking. The bottle was nearly empty. I started to look for clues that Gustav might be the bad guy. For one thing – and this now seems so silly – he looked and smelled odd. Everything about this rescue was odd. Finally, I had to ask myself, 'How odd is it, Miss Smarty-pants? Everything had been odd since I first met Roland Urquardt. And Hank suddenly paying attention to me 'across the crowded room' of the Bridgewater meeting room? I didn't even ask him – ever – what he was doing there. He wasn't a Bridgewater resident. Now I think he was scouting for me, Urquardt's neighbor. They were using me. They probably left messages or signs for each other."

I didn't argue with her. Deborah was a pretty woman. Hank must have been attracted. But if I said that, it would have been just a band-aid on that huge wound in her heart. And I didn't know if it was the truth. I let Deborah keep on talking.

"Hank's suicide. There was nothing to explain it. Roland's murder." She hardly could shape the words. "I was a disaster zone. But nothing seemed to connect. Except the pigeon. Hank had a pigeon. Roland had a pigeon. I wondered a lot about that. I said something to Hank, told him I would like to introduce him to another pigeon-person. But Hank never wanted to meet Roland. Little did I know."

"What about the fire?" I wanted a quick summing up and to see her smile again. Her future with Gustav looked bright.

"When the man who brought my food came again I asked if he would build a fire in the fireplace. He came back with three logs, just enough to last to bedtime. He lit the fire and left. I slept on the sofa wrapped in the blankets, but woke up with a headache. There was smoke in the room. I opened the door. Two men came rushing toward me. One was Gustav. He pushed me aside making angry noises."

"I said, 'I thought you were supposed to be calm,' and he just stared at me with his blue eyes. It chilled my blood. He then walked around the cottage turning on fans and opening windows. When he came back I apologized. I told him I was sorry, that I don't know much about fireplaces."

"He said, 'It's all right now, the fire's out. I'll bring you some more blankets.' When he didn't return after fifteen minutes or so, I noticed he'd left his jacket. I felt in the pockets. Inside was a wallet. I counted the money; it was hundreds. I slipped some of it out before he came back with a big stack of blankets. Then he picked up his jacket and left. My plan was to run away, catch a bus back to Florida – or somewhere."

Deborah seemed to be 'telling all,' but I wished Sam was here to listen and judge whether or not it could be true.

"So I fell in and out of sleep until I realized I was still shivering. I stared at the cold, gray fireplace. I got up and poured myself the last of the bourbon and it made me feel a little warmer. Then I saw a small spark in the grate. If I narrowed my eyes, the spark would dance. I looked around me and found a balled-up tissue between the cushions. I tossed it toward the spark, but it landed short. I got up and pushed it in and it flickered and went out. While I was up I remembered there was food in the refrigerator that I hadn't eaten. The sandwiches were on a paper plate. I ate them now, then rolled the plate into a tube and touched it to the ashes where the spark had been. It started burning and curling until it died out. I pulled out what was left, tore it into small pieces, making lots of ragged edges. This time the fire was about the size of a baseball. I threw in the sofa pillow. It didn't do anything. I went to the kitchen and found a scissors in the utensil drawer. I cut just the pillow cover in strips and laid them across the ashes. The material melted in a sensational green snake of fire. I found this entertaining, so I did it with the other pillow cover and then threw in all the pillow stuffing. It made a warm fire that lasted several minutes."

"I guess I was pretty drunk. I had an idea. I went to the bedroom and pulled the curtains down. I dragged these to the living room, cut and ripped, until I had a whole mountain of cloth. I tied strips together and I put the front end in the fire, and then ran my long snake around the cottage, leaving part of it in every room. The end in the fireplace seemed to die out. I thought maybe the cloth was too cold, or fire retardant. Then suddenly it caught fire and traveled out of the fireplace and onto the hooked rug, marking a charred trail almost to my feet. That's when I sobered up."

"I began to look for an open window on the far end of the house. The one in the bathroom was easy to push outward about five feet off the floor. Using a chair from the kitchen, I was able to climb onto the sill and slip over the edge onto the ground that faced the stables. There was no one in sight. I could see the woods behind me about the distance between your house and mine. But first I walked to the stables and found some horse blankets and wrapped straw in them. I lined them up until they reached back to the cottage. I made sure the fire attached itself to the first roll of straw and kept going. Then I walked away, toward the woods."

"Deborah! How could you? Then how did you and Gustav get to be friends?"

"He was waiting for me on the other side of the woods. He and his helper had been watching me all this time."

"They didn't try to stop you or put the fire out?"

"No. Gus said it probably was the right thing to do. It was 'ordained.' He was packed and ready to go. He knew the police would come."

"You mean he didn't care if the whole place went up in flames? "

"You heard him say that it still belonged in the family. No one would lose anything but himself. And he could afford to rebuild. He said he wasn't even going to claim damages. He'd admit to the accident, calling it a party, and take full responsibility."

"No one was hurt?"

"Only eight people lived on the ranch. He made them leave right away. Their quarters were on the opposite side of the main house from where I was in the cottage, so they had plenty of time to get their belongings together."

"The newspaper didn't report any of this. The implication was that it was arson."

"Well, of course. Anyone would think that."

I thought to myself that the papers had gotten two sensational headlines out of this, one when the circumstances surrounding the fire were still mysterious; the other when the wealthy religious leader explained what happened to the police. I would have to check into the second report. Would it have mentioned Deborah? I bet myself she had told them everything she just told me. Then I remembered the horses that had been mentioned in the paper.

"What about the horses?" I asked Deborah.

"Gustav said he got them all out and herded them to a neighbor."

"But the paper said there were . . ." I stopped. I didn't want her to know. But now Gustav wasn't looking so good to me. Or maybe he was just protecting Deborah from the knowledge that she had killed these beautiful creatures. More beautiful than a pigeon.

FOURTH WEEK

Friday, July 3

Sam and I met for our usual Friday dinner, this time to debrief. With my assistance, he had been busy all week tying up loose ends. Gustav had given him names and addresses, which he had been given to Gustav by Roland at the start of their collaboration. For reasons unclear to us, they had not been sent on to the CIA. Perhaps Roland wanted his supporters to escape. The wheels of justice were in motion, but it would take a while.

I told Sam the long story Deborah spun the day before she left. He laughed and shook his head. Unless we questioned Gustav, we'd never know if that's the way it really happened. There was no excuse for asking him, anyway. Not only had he been extremely cooperative with the CIA, but he had decided he didn't want the island he had inherited, as the last Trandescant heir. Too much blood had been shed there. He wanted it to be a wildlife refuge. He donated it to the City of Dorado Bay and gave them money to restore it as a natural habitat. The old and newer houses all were being razed. Not even the Historical Society objected. They got the furniture, and some valuable Modern art went to the local museum at last.

Earlier in the week I had found articles that reported Gustav Foucault's explanation of the fire and profiled this "religious leader" or "cult guru," depending on whether the paper was friendly (*Serenidad Siren*) or antagonistic (*Los Angeles Lutheran Times*).

"Do you think Gustav Foucault is the good and caring pastor he proclaims to be?" I asked Sam.

"Don't look a gift horse in the mouth," he said. That sent cold through my limbs as I reflected on the terrible images on the ties and the frightened animals reported caught in the fire.

"I've had enough religion for a while," Sam said when I told him some of the newspapers' juicier details.

"And I'm glad I don't belong to any group or club of any kind," I replied.

"Well, we're a good enough club by ourselves," he answered. "Both meanings." And that was as good a compliment to my contributions to his case as I was going to get.

EPILOGUE

Sunday, February 14, 1999

I kept checking the online *Serenidad Siren* until there was some news about the White Angel Ranch revival. The architect's sketches were reproduced on Valentine's Day. The ground-breaking had occurred for the new compound, with a huge temple at the center – or at least it looked like a temple to me. The reporter said about twenty people were living on the property in a scattering of mobile homes. They had some portables that served as common buildings, and new horse barns. A few photos of the members illustrated their various horse-ranching activities. The one of Gustav made him appear out of the dust like Lawrence of Arabia, but with a white bandana tied around his head in place of the turban. Deborah did not appear anywhere in the two-page spread.

I showed Sam my copy when we met for dinner. He studied it carefully.

"I wonder where Deborah was," I mused, looking over his arm. I realized then that there were no females at all in those pictures, and imagined her in the kitchen with all the other commune women, cooking and cleaning up after the festivities.

"I wouldn't be surprised if you hear from her soon," Sam replied.

"Why do you say that?"

"I heard today that Hank – that is, Norris' estate was settled, and that he left two million or so for his old girlfriend. The house belongs to the CIA. The ex-wife gets the house back in Jersey. The daughter and Deborah split the rest, and it was quite a tidy sum he had stashed away."

"Isn't that ironic," I said. "Now she has money and she doesn't need it."

"We don't know that," he replied flatly.

Saturday, May 1, 1999

May Day used to be a time when schoolchildren made cone-shaped baskets out of doilies, filled them with candy and paper flowers, and hung them on doorknobs. Usually it was the older people they gave these treats to. It was a kind, gentle thing to do, and I don't know why teachers don't have them do it any more. Who was going to put a May Basket on my doorknob? There wasn't even a school in our neighborhood.

I was feeling very sorry for myself. Not a lot had happened

since we solved the Urquardt case, unless you counted the sale of all those Shady Lane Properties houses near us, and the election of a good-looking early retiree to the chairmanship of our HOA. Sam still had me helping him with research, but none of the recent criminals were nearly as exciting and deserving of punishment as the avengers. Our Friday night dinner discussions had become more personal, often exchanges about family members, my neighbors, and his colleagues. Jim Purcell was dating the reporter. The wildlife refuge was dedicated. Sam was counting the days until his retirement, still two years away.

Then I received a call from Wendy, owner of the Rose Queen B&B in Pasadena. At first I thought it was a marketing call. The annual mystery writers' conference was scheduled for the following month and I had not made my room reservation. Then I remembered I had had to confess to Wendy that I wasn't a writer, just an amateur sleuth, a modern-day Miss Marple, but less able than she was to outsmart detectives. I should have called her long ago to let her know the outcome. But Wendy wasn't calling to find out about Deborah. She was calling to tell me she had spotted Deborah in the L.A. salon where she now went for her haircuts. I smiled first of all at the prospect that Wendy of the shaggy ponytail had changed her style to something less, well, more polished.

Then the significance of what she was telling me sank in.

"She's a hairdresser now?'

"No, indeed. She was getting a weave. In fact, she looked very good. Designer jeans, red leather jacket, platform heels. Facial work, I think. And she's lost some weight." She paused. "Mammoth designer handbag. I don't think it was a fake."

"Are you sure it was Wendy?"

"Unless she has a younger sister. I know I only saw her for parts of a couple of days when she stayed with us, but I looked at her a lot during that time. And, just like then, when she was done at the salon, a big black limousine came to get her. Then I checked with the receptionist, asked her if the client was named Deborah. She said she was Deborah Foucault, wife of the owner of White Angel Retreat north of Pasadena. She went on to tell me all about the fire, how it used to be a movie star's ranch and then a hippie commune. Apparently now it's a health spa. A kind of spiritual place. Like the ones in Santa Fe. Clients use our salon all the time."

"I guess Serenidad doesn't have one," was all I could say.

"So things turned out all right for her," Wendy suggested. I gave her a brief version of the story as I heard it. She was shocked and delighted, and we promised that I would visit Pasadena one of these days. Robin was coming back to Los Angeles, and with a serious girlfriend he met in Egypt.

I called Sam and told him Wendy's gossip. He just said,

"Anyone can be a pacifist, activist, and live on a commune without taking an oath of poverty."

"At least in California," I had to concede. "Anyway, it's a spiritual retreat now. And a spa. Maybe I should go there."

Right before my bedtime the telephone rang again. I made a mental note to buy a new phone with caller I.D.

"Happy May Day!" I answered, curious to know if the caller even knew what May Day was. This one did, sort of.

"What's wrong, Mom?" Robin asked in his brusque, businesslike voice.

"Nothing at all," I answered.

"But you called out "May Day."

"Never mind, Robin. It's a private joke."

"You remember how many times you told me about the boy who …."

"Called wolf. Yes, I know. I'm in a silly mood."

"Are you having cocktails?"

"Not yet, but maybe I will. Depends on what you called for at this late hour. Are you engaged?"

"I guess I'm pretty transparent – unlike you," he added. "I proposed to Anita. We'd like to be married on New Year's Eve."

"Well! Well!" was all I could say. I imagined a swan-necked Nefertiti. After all, he had been in Cairo for six months and goes back to check on progress.

"Is she an Egyptian girl?" I asked.

"Plain American. I met her in Cairo, though, at a very posh party. I want you two to get to know one another. I'd like Aunt Minnie to meet her, too."

"When?"

"We both can take ten days off in July. That gives Aunt Minnie plenty of warning. You know she'll cook up a storm."

"Let's hope not," I groaned. We talked a little longer and when it was time to hang up, I simply said, "Thanks for the May basket, Robin."

"Wow!" I thought to myself as I lay down in bed. "That year went by in a hurry."

END